# The Heart Sutra

Buddha Shakyamuni

# THE HEART SUTRA
*'Joyous Elegant Speech'*

A Commentary by

## Khenchen Migmar Tsering

**VAJRA**
Publications Inc.Pvt.Ltd.

*Published and Distributed 2025 by*
Vajra Publications Inc.Pvt.Ltd.
Jyatha, Thamel, P.O. Box 21779, Kathmandu, Nepal
Tel.: 977-1-5320562
e-mail: vajrabooksktm@gmail.com
www.vajrabookshop.com

This book was first printed in 2019 at Shiva Offset Press in Dehradun. The printing was sponsored by His Holiness The 42nd and His Holiness The 43rd Sakya Trizin for free distribution at the ceremony to commemorate the 20th year anniversary of the passing of Khenchen Migmar Tsering at the Sakya College in Dehradun.

In accordance with the wish of His Holiness The 42nd Sakya Trizin for this teaching to reach a wider audience, it is now being published by Vajra Publications Inc.Pvt.Ltd. in Nepal.

© 2019 by Sakya Dolma Phodrang. This book is in copyright. No part of this book may be reproduced or utilized in any form or by any means, electronic or mechanical, including photocopying, recording or by any information storage or retrieval system, without permission in writing from Sakya Dolma Phodrang, 192 Rajpur Road, Dehradun, India

Edited and prepared for publication by Kirsty Chakravarty

ISBN 978-9937-624-57-2

Printed by Dongol Printers, Kathmandu, Nepal

# Contents

*Foreword by His Holiness The 42<sup>nd</sup> Sakya Trizin* ....................... vii

*Preface* ............................................................................. viii

*A Short Biography of Khenchen Migmar Tsering* ....................... 1

The Heart Sutra (The Root Text) ........................................... 5

'Joyous Elegant Speech' A Commentary by
    Khenchen Migmar Tsering ............................................. 11

### THE 42ND SAKYA TRIZIN

### FOREWORD

I am very pleased that Khenchen Migmar Tsering's teaching *"Joyous Elegant Speech"* is being made available to Dharma students on the occasion of the 20th anniversary of his passing.

This important commentary on the 'Perfection of Wisdom' by Khenchen Migmar offers an invaluable insight into what is one of the Buddha's most penetrating teachings. The Heart Sutra encompasses the very essence of the Mahayana doctrine, and its elucidation by Khenchen Migmar allows its readers to grasp its deeper meaning.

Khenchen Migmar was a formidable teacher and, as ever, his acute intelligence and profound realisation permeate the pages of the text. We are thankful to Lama Choedak for making this significant teaching accessible to all who wish to deepen their understanding of the Buddhadharma.

Ratna Vajra Sakya
The 42nd Sakya Trizin

20th December 2018

# *Preface*

This is the transcription of an oral commentary on The Heart Sutra taught in English by the Most Venerable Khenchen Migmar Tsering of Sakya College at Sakya Losal Choe Dzong in Canberra during his first teaching visit to Australia in 1993. The audience of this teaching were mainly students of the centre as well as some who had come from other parts of Australia. The atmosphere was delightful and Khenchen Migmar answered questions from the audience after every teaching session.

The Most Venerable Khenchen Migmar Tsering-la was one of the few teachers who possessed the calibre to teach such a profound subject directly in English. The title of this book 'Joyous Elegant Speech' is named after Khenchen Migmar Tsering's ordination name 'Legshey Kunga,' which was given to him by Kyabje Chogye Trichen Rinpoche in 1983.

I would like to thank all those who did a commendable job to listen, transcribe and proof read the manuscript.

I would like to comfort all by sharing this transcription and short biography to remember and honour the late Khenchen Migmar Tsering-la. I thank the current chief abbot Ven. Khenchen Khyenrab Sangpo-la and his assistant abbots and leaders of Sakya College and rejoice in their efforts for taking the initiative to respect and honour The Most Venerable Khenchen Migmar Tsering by celebrating his 20th anniversary on 14th February 2019.

31 October 2018

Lama Choedak Rinpoche
Rongton Buddhist College
Canberra, Australia
Celebration of the Buddha's Descent
From Trayatrimsha Heaven

# A Short Biography of Khenchen Migmar Tsering

Born in western Tibet in 1956, Khenchen Migmar Tsering escaped to India when he was very young. He attended the Central School for Tibetans in Bylakuppe before studying at the Central Tibetan University in Sarnath under Khenpo Rinchen and Tritso Khenpo. He was one of the two students who shared the name 'Migmar' in the Sakya tradition - both came from Bylakuppe. After studying there for several years, he was selected among a group of gifted students to be admitted into the Sakya College, which had been founded by His Holiness The 41st Sakya Trizin, Gongma Trichen Rinpoche and the Most Venerable Khenchen Appey Rinpoche.

He was ordained by Kyabje Chogye Trichen Rinpoche, who gave him the name 'Legshe Kunga'. This name signalled that he was set to become a great teacher of the sacred teachings.

In Sakya College, which was then situated in Mussoorie, Migmar Tsering studied all the eighteen great famous Buddhist philosophical texts according to the Sakyapa tradition under Khenchen Appey Rinpoche. Khenchen Appey Rinpoche highly praised Migmar Tsering's intelligence and depth of understanding. Soon, along with Khenchen Sonam Gyatso, he became the assistant teacher *('kyor-pon')* to Khenchen Appey Rinpoche. Although there were a number of learned students, Khenchen Migmar Tsering and Khenchen Sonam Gyatso were seen as the star students. He was very sharp, intelligent, possessed a deep understanding of the sacred Dharma and was extremely skilful in dealing with people of all walks of life. He was the undoubted successor to Khenchen Appey Rinpoche.

Khenchen Migmar Tsering received Lamdre Tsokshe in 1975 and Lamdre Lobshe in 1980/81 from His Holiness The Sakya Trizin as well as many other empowerments.

Khenchen Migmar Tsering left Sakya College and briefly worked as a translator at the Library of Tibetan Works and Archives in Dharamsala. Following that he was fittingly offered a position of a senior lecturer in the Sakya Buddhist Philosophy Department at the Central Tibetan University in Varanasi. This was welcomed by many academics of the institution. There Khenchen Migmar Tsering obtained the title 'Sakya Khenpo' through his academic credentials and the nature of his work. He became an erudite teacher and scholar, especially with his linguistic skills and his scholarship in the Sakya Tibetan Buddhist philosophy. He taught there for some years and earned the respect from all Traditions for his many qualities. In those days, he was among the rare monks in the Tibetan Buddhist world who could deliver teachings on Buddhist philosophy in English. Therefore, he was invited to travel with Kyabje Chogye Trichen Rinpoche to the USA and Canada as his translator.

In 1989, Khenchen Migmar Tsering was finally appointed and enthroned as the Khenpo at the Sakya College at the behest of His Holiness Sakya Gongma Trichen Rinpoche and Khenchen Appey Rinpoche who at that time was living in Nepal. The role and responsibility of the position of the Khenchen at Sakya College included many hands-on duties. There were no other staff members in those days. His work included administration, supervision of construction work, fund raising and academic duties. The number of students at Sakya College doubled during Khenchen's time.

During Khenchen's time, Sakya College hosted major conferences on Buddhist philosophy attracting many scholars from all over India. Sakya College enjoyed great fame and respect as a well-established centre of serious Buddhist studies. During his role as the Khenpo at Sakya College, some of the most important current leaders of the Sakyapa tradition were his students including The 42$^{nd}$ Kyabgon Sakya Trizin His Holiness Ratna Vajra Rinpoche, Khöndung Gyana Vajra Rinpoche, His Eminence Luding Khenpo, His Eminence Thartse Khenpo, His Eminence Serdhok Tulku, His Eminence Shabdrung Rinchen Paljor, Kyegu Khenchen and many others. Most of the present day Sakya leaders and the Khenpos in Mustang are all students of Khenchen Appey Rinpoche and his sun and moon-like successors.

Unfortunately after a short illness Khenchen Migmar passed away in Dehra Dun on the 14$^{th}$ of February, 1999.

# The Heart Sutra
(The Root Text)

# The Heart Sutra

(The Root Text)

# The Heart of the Transcendent and Victorious Perfection of Wisdom

Prostrations to the Perfection of Wisdom, Mother of the Buddhas of the three times which is unutterable, incomprehensible, inexpressible, unborn, unceasing, the nature of space and the object of the self-cognizant primordial wisdom!

Thus I have heard at one time, the Transcendental Victorious One was abiding at Vulture's Peak in Rajgriha, together with a great assembly of monks and Bodhisattvas. The Buddha being absorbed in a samadhi called 'profound illumination.' At this time Bodhisattva Avalokiteshvara was contemplating the meaning of the profound perfection of wisdom and he understood, he 'saw' that the five aggregates are empty of any inherent existence. Then at that time, through the power and blessing of the Buddha, Shariputra asked Avalokiteshvara: "How should a son of lineage train who wishes to practise the profound perfection of wisdom?" Avalokiteshvara replied to Shariputra, "A son or daughter of lineage who wishes to practise the perfection of wisdom should look at phenomena in this way. They should correctly view the five aggregates as empty of inherent existence. Form is emptiness, emptiness is form, form is not other than emptiness, emptiness is not other than form. So in the same way, feeling, discrimination, compositional factors and consciousness are said to be empty. In this way Shariputra, all phenomena are empty, that is, without characteristic, there is no production, no cessation, they are neither stained or stainless, undiminished or increased. Therefore, Shariputra, because of this, emptiness has no form, no feeling, no discrimination, no compositional factors, no consciousness, it has no eye, no ear, no nose, no tongue, no body, no mind, no form, no sound, no smell, no taste, no tangible object, no phenomenon. It has no eye element up to no mind element. It has no element of eye consciousness up to no element of mind consciousness. It has no ignorance, it has no cessation of ignorance, it has no ageing and death, it has no cessation of ageing and death. It has no suffering, no origin of suffering, no cessation, no path, no transcendental knowledge, no attainment, no non-attainment. Therefore, Shariputra, since Bodhisattvas have no attainment, they depend on the perfection of wisdom and abide in the perfection of wisdom. Since their minds have no obscurations, they have no fear. They have gone beyond all forms of errors or perversity and have attained the ultimate state of nirvana. All the Buddhas of the three times, have by depending on the perfection of wisdom fully realised the perfect, complete and unsurpassed state of enlightenment. Therefore, it is the mantra of perfection of wisdom, the mantra of great knowledge, the unsurpassed mantra, the unequalled mantra, the mantra which pacifies all kinds of sufferings. It is not false, so it should be understood as a true aspect. The Prajnaparamita mantra is proclaimed here and is recited thus: ***Tadyatha Om gate gate paragate parasamgate bodhi svaha.*** Thus, Shariputra, a Bodhisattva Mahasattva, should engage in the practise of this profound perfection of wisdom." Then the Victorious One came out of the absorption of profound illumination and said to Bodhisattva Arya Avalokiteshvara, "Good, it is well done, son of lineage, it is as you have replied. The practise of the perfection of wisdom is as you have explained and the son or daughter of lineage should engage in the practise in just this way and all the Tathagatas will rejoice." After the Victorious one said thus, the Venerable Shariputra, the great Bodhisattva Arya Avalokiteshvara, all the assembly of human disciples, devas, asuras and gandharvas, rejoiced and admired what had just been taught and praised by the Buddha.

I prostrate to the Guru, Buddha, Dharma, Sangha and the Great Mother, Prajnaparamita. Through the power and strength of making prostrations to you all, may these true words of ours be accomplished!

Just as before, when by contemplating the profound meaning of the perfection of wisdom and reciting its words, Indra overcame all the harms of maras, non-humans and so forth, in the same way by our contemplating the profound meaning of the perfection of wisdom and reciting its words, may all the harms towards our spiritual practices such as maras and non-humans be overcome.

May they become non-existent! May they be pacified! May they be thoroughly pacified! Until the accomplishment of perfect enlightenment, I beseech you to thoroughly pacify all the outer and inner obstacles of harm!

May all kinds of interferences, diseases and possessing spirits be pacified. May we be separated from unfavourable conditions and may we achieve favourable conditions and everything excellent. Through this fortune may there be at this time happiness and health!

# 'Joyous Elegant Speech'

A Commentary by
Khenchen Migmar Tsering

# 'Joyous Elegant Speech'

Now first of all create a good motivation, thinking that you are going to engage in this activity of listening to the teaching for the sake of attaining the highest enlightenment, in order to benefit all sentient beings. Remain with this motivation throughout the course of listening to the teaching.

The text we are going to deal with today is the Heart Sutra, which is a Sutra in the Prajnaparamita literature. It is one of the smaller texts among the teachings given by the Buddha on the perfection of wisdom, the highest enlightened wisdom. These teachings on the Prajnaparamita or the Perfection of Wisdom were given mainly at Vultures' Peak in Rajgriha, in what is now Bihar State of India and the teachings come under the category of the second turning of the wheel of the Dharma.

All the teachings of the Buddha are subsumed in the three turnings of the wheel of Dharma. Generally, we say that the first wheel of the four noble truths was turned at Saranath, near Varanasi. The second turning of the wheel was on the teachings based on non-characteristics or teachings based on emptiness and were given mainly at the Vulture's Peak. These teachings were of an analytical nature, while in the first turning of the wheel of Dharma, Buddha mainly taught on the existence of all phenomena on the basis of explaining that one has to accept cause and result in samsara, as well as that which lies within nirvana. In other words, the cause and result of samsara and of nirvana. So these four truths are to be accepted on the basis of the existence of phenomena. In other words the negation of phenomena was not taught in the first turning of the wheel of the Dharma, as the disciples were of the Hinayana level. That teaching was mainly meant for the level of disciples with a lower faculty of mind.

The second turning of the wheel of Dharma, which was called the teaching of non-characteristics, consisted of teachings on emptiness and Prajnaparamita. Now emptiness is taught from the point of view of the object of transcendental knowledge. This is what is to be understood by the teaching on emptiness, whereas Prajnaparamita, or the Perfection of Wisdom, is the transcendental knowledge on the basis of which one understands the state of emptiness. So the Madhyamaka texts that are commentaries to the sutras of the Buddha are also commentaries related to this Prajnaparamita literature. The same Prajnaparamita Sutras, which were taught at Vultures' Peak by the Buddha, have as their commentaries the Madhyamaka literature, as well as the rest of the Prajnaparamita literature. The Prajnaparamita Sutras explicitly show the aspect of emptiness, the object to be realised by the transcendental knowledge, not the levels of realisation. These are said to be taught in the Prajnaparamita Sutras in an implicit way.

Acharya Nagarjuna, who was the foremost expounder of the Madhyamaka literature, the one who first taught the theory of emptiness and in this way began the philosophical school of Madhyamaka, explained the Prajnaparamita Sutras by means of it's explicit meaning. That is, the state of emptiness or the ultimate nature of all phenomena. So Nagarjuna commented on the explicit meaning of the Prajnaparamita Sutras and these texts came to be known as the Madhyamaka literature, Madhyamaka philosophy, whereas, the Bodhisattva Maitreya wrote commentaries on the implicit meaning of the Prajnaparamita literature, which deals with the levels of understanding. With respect to emptiness, which is the object, it is always accompanied by the knowledge that understands that particular level of emptiness.

So there are different levels of establishing this state of emptiness, it is not something that one can see in a moment.

There is no fast method. So these works by Maitreya deal with the gradual method. In the course of this gradual method there will be different levels of object used to establish the state of emptiness and different levels of knowledge of realisation in the course of understanding the state of emptiness. So these different levels of realisation are in connection with the five paths. The realisation of a practitioner at the time of the path of accumulation, the path of application, the path of seeing, the path of meditation and the path of no-more learning are explained in the Prajnaparamita literature.

These texts are called the five teachings of Maitreya, the main text being the Abhisamayalamkara, which is studied as the main subject when it comes to studying the Prajnaparamita literature. The main Prajnaparamita commentary in such a course of study of Prajnaparamita literature would be the Abhisamayalamkara. Now the Madhyamaka literature is a commentary to the same Prajnaparamita literature from a different perspective. You see, the name for the Prajnaparamita Sutras was given on the basis of the knowledge, not on the basis of the object, which is emptiness. But the contents of the Sutras deal with both the object and the subject in implicit and explicit ways. Two systems of commentaries came about in order to explain the broader meaning of the Prajnaparamita Sutras, particularly these commentaries written by Maitreya. Not only the Abhisamayalamkara but also such works as the Sutralamkara, and then the Uttaratantra are also studied as important texts in order to understand the meaning of the Prajnaparamita Sutras.

When the five teachings of Maitreya are explained then some of these texts such as Sutralamkara are said to be commentaries on the Mahayana sutras in general. This means that not only the Prajnaparamita Sutras are appraised, but they also comment on some other sutras, such as the Samadhinirmochana

Sutra, the sutra of explaining the intention of the Buddha. But the Abhisamayalamkara, the Ornament of Realisation, deals particularly with the Prajnaparamita Sutras, which are collected or subsumed in the large, the middle and the concise Prajnaparamita Sutras. Generally, we say the large, the middle and the concise 'mother' literature, which refers to the Prajnaparamita Sutras taught by the Buddha at Vultures' Peak.

Now, to classify the Prajnaparamita Sutras: According to some ancient Tibetan scholars, this literature is classified into two sections: that of mother and son literature, as it is called. The mother literature has six sutras: the large sutra of one hundred thousand verses; one of twenty-five thousand verses; one of eighteen thousand verses and then two others that have more than eight thousand verses. The sixth sutra has a similar number of verses. The main sutras are the one hundred thousand; the twenty-five thousand and the eight thousand verse sutras. There are some sutras that have a few more or less verses. Two others are counted with these main ones and they are classified as the mother Prajnaparamita Sutras. The shorter ones, which also deal with the same subject, are the Prajnaparamita Sutra with seven hundred verses, the sutra of four hundred verses and the other shorter versions of Prajnaparamita, including the Heart Sutra and Vajracchedika Sutra. These are considered as the son literature of Prajnaparamita.

The distinction made between mother and son literature is on the basis of whether all the eight topics are dealt with or not. When it comes to explaining the levels of realisation, then as explained in the Abhisamayalamkara, eight topics are dealt with. Firstly, there are three types of knowledge referred to here, omniscient knowledge, knowledge of path and fundamental knowledge. In fact these are first explained on the basis of the foundation of learning, not in the form of practice. Then, there are four applications that are the actual different levels of realisation that a practitioner will attain in the course of practise. Beginning with the application of complete aspects, which begins with the realisation at the time of accumulation and then comes the application of instantaneous practise which is the realisation at the time of the Bodhisattva on the tenth bhumi, after that, the eighth topic comes, the result which is called the 'Dharmakaya' or the 'Body of Truth'. So the first of these topics is named 'omniscient knowledge', but it is not explained on the basis of being what one will first of all realise or attain. This is mentioned as the first topic, so that one will know about the result of the practise one is going to be engaged in.

When someone sees the benefit or good qualities of an object or aim, which one is wishing to achieve, then naturally they will have joy and happily engage in the method to achieve this result. So for that reason the first topic is called omniscient knowledge. A sutra which deals with all these eight topics is called a mother sutra, whereas the Prajnaparamita Sutra which deals with some but not all of these eight, is considered as son literature.

So we can classify the Prajnaparamita Sutras under these two classifications, but most scholars say that it is not necessary to classify into mother and son sutras, because all Prajnaparamita Sutras can be accepted as mother sutras or mother literature. As in the title of this sutra, the name 'mother' is to symbolise or indicate the transcendental wisdom that is the Prajnaparamita. It is called 'mother' because as a result of this transcendental knowledge, the Bodhisattva arises. One can become a Bodhisattva. One can become a Buddha. In other words, four types of Arya, or superior beings arise as a result of Prajnaparamita, as a result of this transcendental knowledge. So, in accordance with the level of this ultimate knowledge, this Prajnaparamita, a different realisation is attained, or one obtains different results.

Of the three types of knowledge, the knowledge of omniscience is the highest realisation that an Arya Buddha achieves. When it comes to dividing the Arya, or superior being, then we have four types: the Shravaka Arya, Pratyekabuddha Arya, Bodhisattva Arya and Arya Buddha. The Arya in Mahayana is divided into two: Arya Bodhisattva and Arya Buddha. So these four Aryas arise as a result of the perfection of wisdom and the levels of perfection are in the form of the knowledge of omniscience, knowledge of the path and fundamental knowledge. Now of the three types of knowledge explained in the eight topics of Prajnaparamita literature, the fundamental knowledge is the cause of two types of Arya: the Arya Shravaka and Arya Pratyekabuddha. Fundamental knowledge refers to the knowledge that realises the emptiness of the aggregates, which are the basis of the 'self', but does not include the realisation of the emptiness of all phenomena. The knowledge of the path refers to the knowledge of a Bodhisattva that understands all three paths of the three yanas, or vehicles: the path of the Shravaka, of the Pratyekabuddha and the path of a Bodhisattva. This realisation of these three paths is called the knowledge of the path, which is the realisation of the Arya Bodhisattva. The knowledge of omniscience is the knowledge by which one becomes an Arya Buddha. So here, the Prajnaparamita, which is the perfection of wisdom, is divided into these three types of knowledge, as a result of which we have the four types of Arya.

As the perfection of wisdom functions as a cause for the attainment of these four types of Aryas, then the perfection of wisdom is called the mother and the four Aryas are referred to as the sons. That is, the mother refers to the knowledge and the son refers to the Aryas. How a mother produces an Arya as a son is explained from two aspects. This mother is also further divided into the mother who produces an Arya and that which assists the Arya in functioning in his or her activity. The mother which is the producing mother and in a way the benefiting mother is explained in terms of different moments.

For example, the understanding of the aggregates as emptiness on the level of the path of application is also called a mother because in the next moment the one who has realized it will attain the stage or level of Shravaka Arhat. So this Arhat, which arises one moment later than the accumulated fundamental knowledge, is the result of the previous accumulation of this fundamental knowledge. So this fundamental knowledge is the mother with respect to producing the Shravaka Arhat or Arya. So this idea of mother and son with respect to the mother Prajnaparamita producing the Arya is explained in terms of two different moments.

Now the knowledge itself cannot produce the Shravaka Arhat, the one who already possesses this knowledge because this knowledge and the Arya who possesses it exist at the same time. Two things that are simultaneous cannot act as a cause and a result. Cause and result have to be explained in terms of different moments because the cause comes one moment before and the result one moment later. This fundamental knowledge that the Shravaka Arhat possesses cannot become a mother that produces that Arya because they exist at the same time. But as a result of that fundamental knowledge, that Shravaka Arhat can function or engage in his or her particular activity, which is remaining in nirvana.

The Shravaka Arhat can remain in nirvana that is free from the sufferings of samsara because of possessing this fundamental knowledge. So the fundamental knowledge which one possesses now acts as an assistant or a condition by which one remains in nirvana. So it is called the mother of assisting or benefiting. The mother and son relationship is explained in the context of the mother Prajnaparamita producing an Arya or a mother helping an Arya in his or her function. These are the two contexts in which it is explained.

Since the term 'mother' is used to indicate the Prajnaparamita or the perfection of wisdom itself, then to have the name 'mother' for a sutra, it is not necessary that the sutra should deal with all the eight topics because being named mother, the knowledge itself becomes a mother in relation to the four Aryas or superior beings.

So the Heart Sutra is also named a mother sutra because it deals with the topic of Prajnaparamita, which is the mother to all the Aryas. It is also called the mother of all the Buddhas of the three times. It is said in the sutras, as well as in many commentaries that the attainment of Buddhahood by all the Buddhas of three times depends on this Prajnaparamita. So the importance of Prajnaparamita is explained in the different sutras and shastras by saying that only by depending on this Prajnaparamita is one able to become a Buddha. So whether it is the present Buddha, a Buddha in the past or a Buddha yet to come, this result is due only to the Prajnaparamita. This refers not only to the Arya Buddha but also the other three types of Aryas. If the attainment of Buddhahood depends on Prajnaparamita then naturally the attainment of the level of Bodhisattva depends on it as well.

The other two Aryas, the Shravaka Arya and Pratyekabuddha Arya, who are called the Hinayana realisers, those who have attained the Hinayana result, also depend on the Prajnaparamita because as explained earlier, Prajnaparamita consists of these three kinds of knowledge. It does not mean only the omniscient knowledge but all three. As explained earlier, the attainment of the two Hinayana results depends on the fundamental knowledge. In respect of the order of explanation in the text, omniscient knowledge comes first and then the knowledge of path and then the fundamental knowledge.

So, the fundamental knowledge is the knowledge of the two Hinayana realisers, without attaining or gaining this knowledge one cannot become a Hinayana realiser. The attainment of Hinayana result definitely depends on the Prajnaparamita. To gain any kind of realisation or attainment, in any of the three yanas, whether it is Shravakayana or Pratyekabuddhayana, or Mahayana, Prajnaparamita becomes indispensable. It is because of this that it is considered very important.

This particular sutra, the Heart Sutra, is of particular importance because it is concise and very short with respect to the number of words but it has all the meaning explained that one could find in the large, middle and concise Prajnaparamita Sutras. The large sutra of one hundred thousand verses has twelve volumes in the Tibetan translation, the middle-sized sutra of twenty-five thousand verses has three volumes and the concise sutra of eight thousand verses has one volume. The same meaning can be found in the Heart Sutra as is contained in the large sutra of one hundred thousand verses.

Whenever there is more than one sutra on the same subject, there is an argument about the purpose of the other sutras. It is argued that there is no need for repetition; if a meaning is taught in one sutra then another sutra on the same subject seems superfluous. This argument is also applicable to the commentaries. The Buddha gave all kinds of teachings in the sutras, there is no other form or method that the Buddha did not teach, so there won't be any special meaning or content in the commentaries, it is argued.

However, as there are people with different levels of mental faculties, so a particular teaching can be understood by one person but cannot be understood by another. This is due to the different levels of their mind. A teaching that a practitioner of a particular level may understand at one point in time may not be understood by a practitioner on the same level at another point in time.

So in order to enable people of different levels of mind to understand the meaning explained in the sutras, the commentaries are written. Those who have a natural inclination towards lengthier explanations will find the longer Prajnaparamita helpful. Those of sharper mental faculties, who do not have a natural inclination for lengthier explanations but strive for the meaning and those who have the intellect to understand, will find such sutras as this Heart Sutra more beneficial.

It is for these reasons that all Tibetan Buddhists in all the Tibetan monasteries consider the Heart Sutra so important. All monks recite it regularly, whenever a religious function commences it is usual that it begins with the recitation of the Heart Sutra. This is followed by another ritual prayer, which is recited to dispel obstacles.

Generally, the benefit of the recitation of this Sutra, which is applicable to the chanting of all sutras, is the accumulation of merit. The chanting of even one verse of Dharma that was taught by the Buddha, in this case, the Heart Sutra, has great merit, as one is expressing the ultimate meaning of Prajnaparamita. The mind will also focus on the meaning of the words. Even if one does not understand the meaning of the words one still accrues merit. There will be others who hear the chanting of the words, thereby naturally imprinting on their minds what they hear. By helping others in this way, one also accumulates merit. So the chanting of this sutra is a common traditional practise in Tibetan monasteries.

When we explain the Prajnaparamita in its direct application, we divide it into three sections: causal Prajnaparamita, resultant

Prajnaparamita and textual Prajnaparamita. The word paramita literally means that which has gone beyond, and prajna means transcendental wisdom, the ultimate knowledge. So, 'the knowledge that has gone beyond' is the literal meaning of Prajnaparamita. It is only the omniscient knowledge of the Buddha that has gone beyond the limits of samsara and nirvana, which is the exact meaning of Prajnaparamita. The word Prajnaparamita can be used on different levels but the actual Prajnaparamita is to be understood in terms of resultant Prajnaparamita. The causal Prajnaparamita is all the knowledge which the realisers of all three yanas possess, like the knowledge of path, which is, as was explained earlier, only a cause by which one will obtain the omniscient knowledge, it is not the result.

There are two levels to this, the knowledge at the time of the path of accumulation and that at the time of the path of application. This is not as direct as the knowledge one has as an Arya but it is still considered as Prajnaparamita. All the texts, the sutras dealing with Prajnaparamita as well as the commentaries (shastras), are called textual Prajnaparamita. A text, for instance, this Heart Sutra, is not 'the knowledge that has gone beyond samsara and nirvana', so it is not the definitive, or actual Prajnaparamita. It is however named Prajnaparamita because it expresses this; it deals with the subject of Prajnaparamita.

When the word 'mother' is used, it is generally more pervasive in meaning than the word Prajnaparamita. Prajnaparamita refers solely to the omniscient knowledge whereas mother can even refer to the knowledge of the path, the knowledge that a Bodhisattva and the other lower Aryas possess. This knowledge functions as a cause, functions as a mother to produce these realisers or Aryas. As they are still in the process of attaining the highest enlightenment, their knowledge does not fit the definition of 'the knowledge that has gone beyond'.

A text does not have the definition of a 'mother' either. A text cannot produce an Arya; one will not become an Arya because of the text. Neither will the text assist in the functioning of an Arya. However, because it deals with the topic of mother Prajnaparamita or the knowledge that is the 'mother,' it is also called Prajnaparamita.

So these explanations are in relation to the naming of things as Prajnaparamita. There are instances of giving the name of the result to the cause, giving the name of the cause to the result, giving the name of the expressed meaning to the expression and giving the name of the expression to the expressed meaning. When we say 'sun' referring to the sun's rays, the light rays of the sun, then the name 'sun' is given to the sun's rays on the strength of the name of a cause being given to the result. The sun's rays are the result of the sun; they are not the actual sun. So here we have an example of the name of a cause being given to the result. Similarly, when the name Prajnaparamita is given to the knowledge of the lower Aryas, it is done on the strength of giving the name of the result to the cause. The Prajnaparamita is the result, not the cause. When dealing with the text, it is named on the basis of giving the name of the meaning to the words; it is named because of the relationship between the expressed meaning and the expression.

In the Tibetan text, the sutra begins with the Sanskrit title, *Bhagavati prajnaparamita hridaya*, which translates as:

*The Heart of the Transcendent and Victorious Perfection of Wisdom.*

As in every Tibetan sutra or shastra, it always begins with the Sanskrit title, firstly to show that this is an original teaching of the Buddha who gave the original teaching in the Sanskrit language and secondly, as it has been translated from Sanskrit, we must remember the kindness of the translators who have translated it into Tibetan, in this case.

Then comes the title translated into Tibetan. The purpose of having a title is that just from this, one can have a glimpse of the meaning of the text that one is going to study. Prajnaparamita has already been explained. Heart or essence (*hridaya*), is used in the title as this sutra contains the essential meaning of all the other Prajnaparamita Sutras. *Bhagavati*, the feminine of *Bhagavat*, is translated as transcendent and victorious and in some other works as the Blessed One, she who has transcended both the extremes of samsara and nirvana. By getting rid of the sufferings of samsara one has gone beyond samsara and the one with omniscient knowledge does not remain in the pacified state of nirvana, in order to work for the benefit of sentient beings. This state is called victorious because it has destroyed the four maras, the four negative forces: the *devaputra* mara (the demon of the god's son), *skhanda* mara (the demon of the aggregates), *klesha* mara (the demon of the delusions) and *mriti* mara (the demon of death.) Mara refers to a negative force that acts as an obstacle to the achievement of the highest enlightenment. *Devaputra* mara is associated with evil spirits, a particular type of deva being, who because of their previous karma cause obstacles and hindrances to anyone who is engaged in a virtuous activity. If the merit of the practitioner is not strong enough, then there is the chance of obstacles coming during the performance of a good activity. This happens even in ordinary cases. If you don't look further than a direct cause and result of an activity, then one may think one is doing very good things, accumulating virtuous merit but still one faces many problems, whereas those who are indulging in non-virtuous activities, very sinful activities, seem to be prospering in their daily lives. It is not guaranteed that a good action will have an immediate result, neither is it guaranteed that the one who is performing the good action is strong enough to drive away the obstacles. One may have good motivation and perform a good activity but one may require another quality to conquer the obstacles. One must have accumulated the necessary merit from previous lifetimes.

In Vajrayana, there are many methods mentioned to deal with different obstacles. The destruction of the obstacles is not the main objective but in order to reach the highest enlightenment these need to be overcome. When one becomes an enlightened being, one has overcome all of these *devaputra* mara obstacles. Through practice, when one is able to get rid of all one's delusions of hatred, desire and ignorance, the sufferings of samsara, this means that one has destroyed the mara of delusions. As long as one has these delusions, one cannot have the ultimate state of enlightenment. One cannot progress in one's practice because the delusions will obstruct one's way.

After one has attained Buddhahood, because one has gone beyond the cycle of birth and death in samsara, one is no longer under the influence of uncontrolled death. The realiser has more control over death than death has control over the realiser. In the case of an ordinary sentient being, death has control. When the time of death comes, nobody has a chance to escape from death, or postpone it. In the case of an enlightened being, one can perform the activity of passing away or dying, whenever one wishes. Coming in the form of a human being, one can have the lifespan one wishes; one can lengthen one's lifespan according to one's wish. In the case of Shakyamuni Buddha, it is said that he lengthened his lifespan by three months. As he had destroyed the mara of death, he had control over death and was able to postpone the occurrence of death.

When one passes into the nirvana of no remainder, when an enlightened being shows the manifestation of dying, he or she discards the five aggregates and is said to have destroyed the mara of the aggregates, which will not occur again. An ordinary sentient being at the time of death discards the five aggregates of this life but because he or she has not got rid of the entire cycle of birth and death, there will be a new set of five aggregates in the next life. Because of a Buddha's possession of the transcendental, omniscient knowledge, which is the Prajnaparamita, he is said to have overcome the four maras. Thus the Buddha is victorious.

There are different ways of giving a title to a sutra or shastra. Sometimes the title is given on the basis of the number of verses in the particular text: for example, 'The Prajnaparamita with One Hundred Thousand Verses'. This type of title is called the title given on the basis of expression. Another way of giving a title can be on the basis of who requested the teaching. For example, the *Upaliparipriccha* Sutra, the sutra requested by *Upali*, the *Indraparipriccha* Sutra, the sutra requested by *Indra*. These are sutras, particular teachings given by the Buddha at the request of a certain disciple. Another way of giving a title can be on the basis of the name of the place, or the circumstances under which the particular sutra was given, for example, the Lankavatara Sutra, the sutra given while travelling to Sri Lanka.

Generally, the title is given from the context of the content of the text as in this case here. The text is divided into three sections. The first part is the homage or salutations by the translator, the second part, the actual text followed by the third part, the conclusion.

The homage or salutations is paid to the Prajnaparamita itself. The translator inserted the homage; it is not part of the original Sanskrit sutra itself. In order to accomplish the task of translation and in order to show that the translators are noble beings, they always pay homage to a holy being or a holy quality. By paying homage to a holy being or quality, in this case the Prajnaparamita, merit will be accrued and this merit will enable one to accomplish the task of translation without obstacle. In the shastras or commentaries, there will usually be two lines of salutation. One is by the translator and one is by the author of the commentary. The explanation of the actual text has two outlines. The first is the background of the teaching of this sutra, which is again divided into two, the common background and the uncommon background.

The second outline is the main bulk of the teaching itself. This first section is to be found in all of the Buddha's sutras, particularly those sutras related to the Vinaya, teachings on the moral discipline of those who have taken vows. The circumstances under which the Buddha gave these teachings are mentioned at the beginning of the teachings and these serve as the background. The text states,

*Thus I have heard at one time, the Transcendental Victorious One was abiding at Vulture's Peak in Rajgriha, together with a great assembly of monks and Bodhisattvas.*

This is the common background. All the teachings of the Buddha were collected later by his disciples, the Arhats. Soon after the parinirvana, the passing away of the Buddha, all the remaining Arhats gathered at Rajgriha.

Upali, Kasyapa and Ananda mainly collected the teachings of the Buddha and this was the origin of what is known as the 'Tripitaka', the three baskets of the teachings. The teachings that deal with transcendental wisdom are known as the Abhidharma Pitaka. The teachings that deal with meditation or absorption (samadhi), are called the Sutra Pitaka. The teachings that deal with the moral discipline of those who have taken vows, novice and fully ordained bhikshus and bhikshunis, are called the Vinaya Pitaka. Arhat Kasyapa, who was the first of the seven successors of the Buddha who are listed, was responsible for collecting the Abhidharma Pitaka. The Arhat Ananda compiled the Sutra Pitaka, while Arhat Upali collected the Vinaya Pitaka. When they collected these teachings, it was in the form of recitation rather than putting them into written form. There are several different versions of how the teachings of the Buddha first came to be written down in book form but the first collection of the teachings was obtained by the chanting of all the teachings by these three Arhats.

This is the reason why all the sutras begin with the phrase, *'Thus I have heard at one time'*, because the Arhat is reciting the words which the Buddha taught at a certain time and a certain place. So this sutra is said to have been collected by Ananda. As it deals with transcendental knowledge it can be considered as part of the Abhidharma Pitaka but the distinction as to which sutras are in which pitaka is not that definite, because one sutra can deal with all three topics.

Any sutra that is explained through question and answer between the Buddha and one of his disciples, or between two of his disciples, is called the 'Sutra Pitaka', the basket of discourses. This Heart Sutra expresses the Prajnaparamita through a dialogue between Shariputra and the Bodhisattva Avalokiteshvara, Shariputra being one of the main disciples among the Hinayana practitioners and Avalokiteshvara, one of the main disciples among the Mahayana practitioners. This dialogue took place in front of the Buddha, under his direct supervision, as a direct blessing of the Buddha, so the teachings that have come from this are considered to be the teachings of the Buddha. When Ananda recited this sutra it was reporting an account of part of Buddha's life.

Generally, we divide the teachings of the Buddha into three categories: (a) permitted teachings, (b) blessed teachings and (c) teachings spoken directly. Permitted teachings are those teachings in the sutras not directly spoken by the Buddha but have been blessed as the teaching of the Buddha, such as those that commence, *'Thus I have heard at one time.'* Now this line was not actually spoken by the Buddha but in the course of his teachings, Buddha himself said that after his parinirvana, when the teachings needed to be collected, this was the form they should take. He directed his students to compile the teachings in this manner.

Blessed teachings are the actual conversations of his disciples, such as the question put by Shariputra or the answer given by Avalokiteshvara. These were not the direct teachings of the Buddha but the Buddha was said to have blessed them. The blessed teachings of the Buddha can cover such things as all the different types of miracles performed by a Pratyekabuddha.

It is even more applicable to the Bodhisattvas, as they work for the benefit of all types of sentient beings; they pursue all types of methods, sometimes teaching directly, sometimes through another person, sometimes enabling inanimate objects to give out the 'sound of the Dharma.'

An example of this is the drum in the Thirty-third Heaven, which occasionally makes the sound that is called the four seals of the teachings.

(i) That all compounded things are impermanent
(ii) Everything that deteriorates is suffering
(iii) Nirvana is peace
(iv) All phenomena are selfless and empty.

One can obtain the same meaning from the sound of this drum that one can get by hearing a teaching expressed through the mouth. These are considered as the different methods of teaching used by the Buddhas and Bodhisattvas for the sake of subduing disciples.

Spoken teaching is those words in the sutras that were directly uttered by the Buddha, such as the section in the Heart Sutra after the dialogue between Avalokiteshvara and Shariputra, where Buddha praised Avalokiteshvara, saying that his reply to Shariputra was exact and perfect.

At the time when the Buddha was turning the second wheel of the Dharma, the Prajnaparamita teachings at Vulture's peak in Rajgriha, simultaneously through a miraculous form, he is said to have been giving another teaching on Vajrayana at another place. Vulture's Peak, which is still called this today, in present day Rajgriha, is where Buddha gave a whole series of teachings; the second wheel turning of the Dharma was not only for one day or one session. So the compilation of teachings called the second wheel turning was given on different occasions, this division was made mainly on the basis of the subject, which deals with non-characteristics, or ultimate emptiness.

The place mentioned in connection with the third wheel turning of the Dharma, when the Buddha taught the Vajrayana, is usually Vasali, in the present day State of Bihar but this is not the only place specified. Otherwise, one may assume that Buddha only taught at these three places, Saranath, Vulture's Peak and Vasali but this is not so. He also taught at Sravasti, which is a very important holy place in the present state of Uttar Pradesh. Buddha is said to have spent twenty-three rainy season retreats there.

The disciples of Buddha included both Hinayana and Bodhisattva practitioners. When the text says, '*surrounded by a large assembly of bhikshus*', it mainly refers to these Hinayana disciples. To the appearance of the outer world, we say that most of his disciples were Hinayana practitioners, such as Shariputra and Maudgaliyaputra, who were considered the two most excellent disciples of the Buddha, like the right and left sides of the Buddha. This does not mean that there were not Mahayana disciples present. '*There were also many Bodhisattvas*', like Avalokiteshvara, for example.

Shariputra and Maudgaliyaputra were initially followers of another religion. In the case of Shariputra, it is said that the Buddha ordained him as a Bikshu, through the method of calling his name. There are ten different methods mentioned in the Vinaya, by which a person can be ordained as a Bikshu. At the present time, there is only one method left, which is the ritual practised in both the Theravada and Mahayana systems. The Vinaya rules of Sarvastivada and Theravada are both still extant and both of these systems have only one method of ordaining someone, which is through the ritual. At the time of Buddha, there were nine other methods, including this 'calling by name' method. When the karmic link had been formed between Shariputra and the Buddha and had ripened, then when the Buddha met Shariputra, by merely saying, "Shariputra come here", it is said that he was immediately ordained as a monk, there was no need to go through a ritual.

There was another method called 'ordination by correspondence'. A certain female disciple of the Buddha wanted very much to be ordained as a nun, but was unable to physically come to where Buddha was at the time. She wrote to the Buddha about her intentions, the Buddha replied by letter and in this way she was said to have been ordained.

These ancient methods of ordination are only applicable to disciples with certain levels of mind. Their faith and intention had to be very strong. In the case of the Prajnaparamita Sutra of eight thousand verses and most of the other more extensive texts, the teaching is explained through a dialogue between the Buddha and Subhuti. With the Heart Sutra however, we have Shariputra having a dialogue with Avalokiteshvara. Included in the Bodhisattva disciples are, what are called, the eight close sons of the Buddha: Avalokiteshvara, Manjushri, Vajrapani, Kshitigarbha, Akashagarbha, Samantabadhra, Nivaranavishkhambhin and Maitreya. So these great Bodhisattvas all came to receive teachings from the Buddha at one time or another. Sometimes, they attended teachings together or at other times alone, depending on the circumstance. In this case, Avalokiteshvara was said to have been present.

There is no mention, in the sutra, of Avalokiteshvara being in the form of a man, like Shariputra, for example. There is mention of the life story of Shariputra, from the time of his birth to his meeting with the Buddha but Bodhisattvas, such as Avalokiteshvara, do not remain in one place like other people but generally reside in their own Buddha realm. However, as they are still in the course of practice as a Bodhisattva, whenever there are teachings, whether they are being held in the Buddha realm of Shakyamuni Buddha or of Amitabha Buddha that is called Sukhavati, then they would travel there to receive them. So these Bodhisattvas come to receive the teachings of the Buddha and also act as a medium between the Buddha and the assembly of other disciples.

In this case, the realisation of a Mahayana Bodhisattva is greater than the realisation of the majority of the assembly of Hinayana bhikshus, so the Bodhisattva could make them understand more clearly what the Buddha taught. As was explained earlier, the Bodhisattva assists the process through the blessing of the Buddha. There are several different opinions as to whether Shariputra was a real Shravaka or Hinayana disciple, or whether he was an emanation of a Buddha or a Bodhisattva. Usually, in the final analysis, Shariputra is considered to be an emanation of a Buddha.

There are three types of Hinayana realiser: a real Hinayana realiser, a Hinayana realiser who is an emanation of a Bodhisattva and a Hinayana realiser who is an emanation of a Buddha. Sometimes a Bodhisattva, in order to benefit a certain group of disciples, will manifest in the form of a Shravaka, a Hinayana realiser. Similarly, sometimes a Buddha will do likewise. Not only Shariputra but also many of the disciples of the Buddha, are considered to be emanations of various Buddhas, who collectively work for the benefit of all sentient beings.

Through the practice of prayer, Bodhisattvas request that when there is a need for a Shravaka disciple, for instance, may they take rebirth as such a disciple. Whenever there is the need for a bridge at a certain place, for example, they may take rebirth as a bridge. Through countless aeons these prayers have been offered with great faith and strength of practice, so at the time of the attainment of an Arya Bodhisattva and particularly after the attainment of Buddhahood, all these prayers become ultimately accomplished. Only one Buddha manifested as the Shakyamuni Buddha, as it is said that on the occasion of one teaching of the Buddha, there is only one Buddha to be found. Within the time frame of the existence of the teachings of the Buddha Shakyamuni, which is generally considered to be five thousand years, there will not be another Buddha who will be the main teacher, though there may be various manifestations on other levels.

In this period there may be many Bodhisattvas, who as a result of the completion of their practise, become Buddhas but they are not considered as the main teacher or Buddha. Where there can be slight differences with respect to understanding and the degree of abandonment of realisers on different levels, there is no difference in the enlightenment and understanding of all the Buddhas of the three times. Any Buddha can perform the same activities that another Buddha is capable of but with respect to the circumstances where different types of activities are required, then some may come in the form of disciples while some may come as householders who help the Sangha of the Buddha. We usually consider Avalokiteshvara, Manjushri and the other great eight Bodhisattvas to have already attained Buddhahood long ago but due to their prayers to benefit sentient beings until the end of samsara, they manifest in the form of Bodhisattvas.

In the case of Manjushri, as an embodiment of transcendental wisdom, there is a very special link between him and all types of knowledge. He is considered as the deity, the Bodhisattva, through which one can obtain all types of knowledge in the least time. Avalokiteshvara, of course, embodies the compassion of all the Buddhas collectively. In the common background, is included what are called the five auspicious factors, which are also applicable to all auspicious rituals and occasions. When the auspicious factors of teacher, time, place, disciples and teaching are present, then it will become a complete occurrence of auspiciousness, there being no reason for failure.

So here, the Transcendental Victor, the Buddha, is the teacher, who gave the Heart Sutra. He is not an ordinary type of teacher who has not abandoned his own faults and delusions, making it impossible to give a perfect, stainless teaching. The teacher as the Buddha is considered the auspicious teacher. It is generally considered that the Buddha was around fifty-seven when he gave this teaching. The factor of time is not explicitly mentioned but it is said that Buddha had returned from Vasali to Vulture's peak, so this is considered as the auspicious factor of time. Vulture's Peak in Rajgriha is considered a very auspicious place, as due to the Buddha already having given many teachings on Prajnaparamita, it had become a very blessed place. The general version of how the place got its name is that when the Buddha gave teachings at one time, many Bodhisattvas came to listen in the form of vultures circling overhead.

The assembly of monks and Bodhisattvas is considered to be the auspicious disciples. They were not just ordinary disciples who cannot gain much benefit from the teaching but a collection of the most excellent disciples. The auspicious teaching comes later in the text when Avalokiteshvara starts to answer Shariputra, as it deals with the most essential part of the Buddha's teachings - transcendental knowledge. So these five factors are present in this Heart Sutra.

The uncommon background begins with a description:

*The Buddha being absorbed in a samadhi called 'profound illumination.' At this time Bodhisattva Avalokiteshvara was contemplating the meaning of the profound perfection of wisdom and he understood, he 'saw' that the five aggregates are empty of any inherent existence.*

Simultaneously, by the power of the Buddha, Shariputra was moved to ask Bodhisattva Avalokiteshvara about how to practise.

As far as the assembled monks and Bodhisattvas are concerned there is no external distinguishing characteristic of the 'profound illumination' from the general samadhi of realising ultimate emptiness. Within this usual transcendental absorption of the Buddha, many different types of meditation are mentioned. In the case of a Bodhisattva on the last bhumi level, then just before attaining Buddhahood, one enters into an absorption called 'vajra-like samadhi'. There is no difference in the nature of any type of absorption where the realiser remains in the state of ultimate emptiness. However as a result of this state, different activities will arise. So the absorptions have been given different names.

When we talk about 'compassion' and 'bodhicitta', there are different definitions of these mental states but in the case of the aforementioned absorptions, it is only because each will function as a cause for a certain activity related to other disciples that they are differentiated by name. The samadhi which the Buddha entered into in this case, in order to function as the cause to begin the dialogue between the two disciples is this 'profound Illumination'. It is said that outwardly, Buddha radiated brilliant light rays from his body, while he was remaining in this meditation. These light rays and the manner in which he was absorbed in meditation were not comprehended or perceived by all the disciples present. Certain higher levels of disciple, such as the Bodhisattvas only understood this. So this is also part of the uncommon background, as all those present did not share it. Whenever a teaching was given, it is said that the Buddha remained in one or another particular samadhi. In this case, Buddha was said to have remained in this absorption until the dialogue between Avalokiteshvara and Shariputra came to an end. This does not mean that he was so deep in meditation that he was not aware of what was going on between the two disciples. This is another uncommon characteristic of the state of Buddhahood.

In the case of a realiser or Bodhisattva on the path, when one enters into the state of deep meditation, one is not aware of the activities outside of that meditation session. When one is in the post-meditative state and engaged in different activities, then one cannot remain in any type of absorption. These two states will come at different times but not simultaneously. In the case of a Buddha, however, there is no occasion when he does not remain in meditative equipoise.

While a Buddha remains absorbed inside, as it were, simultaneously other activities can be engaged in, such as dealing with disciples. So the Buddha was aware of the dialogue and the assembly of disciples. The purpose of remaining in this absorption is to show that the following teaching is an object of the understanding a Buddha has while in absorption. It is not a teaching that can be understood just by listening to it or by contemplation. The reason Buddha's body radiated brilliant lights was to suppress the natural light that emanates from the bodies of devas. It is said that whenever a Buddha gives a teaching, not only does the assembly constitute human beings but god beings from the Thirty-third Heaven or Tushita Heaven also participate. From birth, these god beings radiate light from their bodies. It is explained that in the Thirty-third Heaven, for example, there is no need of external illumination, such as the sun and the moon. As a result of this quality, when they come to the teachings in the human realm, they have a certain pride about being superior to human beings, who do not have these radiations. When a certain disciple has these delusions, pride in this case, then they will not be a suitable vessel for receiving the teachings, their mental continuum will not be in a state where they can grasp the teachings properly.

To destroy this pride, the Buddha radiated such brilliant light rays from his body that the god beings realized that compared to his, their light rays were nothing. The god beings were humbled and thus became perfect disciples to receive the teaching. Because of the blessing of the Buddha, Bodhisattva Avalokiteshvara naturally contemplated on the meaning of the profound perfection of wisdom, the transcendental wisdom realising ultimate truth. At this time he also understood the emptiness of the five aggregates. On the basis of this knowledge, he was able to give replies to the questions put by Shariputra.

Avalokiteshvara is described by three appellations in the text, that of Bodhisattva Mahasattva and Arya. The term Bodhisattva is explained from two points of view. Firstly, as soon as anyone generates the mind of enlightenment, bodhicitta, the mind that wishes to attain Buddhahood for the sake of all sentient beings, then they are called a 'Bodhisattva'. Shantideva said in the Bodhisattvacharyavatara that, as long as one produces this kind of mind, one can be called a Bodhisattva, the child of the Tathagata and one will become an object of respect by all beings of the six realms, even if one is in the midst of the cycle of birth and death, residing in samsara.

The criterion for entering the Mahayana path is also based on the generation of bodhicitta.

Secondly, it is said in the Madhyamakavatara that when one attains the first bhumi and becomes an Arya, in terms of Mahayana practise, only then can one be called a Bodhisattva. The differentiation here is in relation to the generation of ultimate bodhicitta. These two ways of defining a Bodhisattva are in relation to the two types of bodhicitta - relative and ultimate. Conventional or relative bodhicitta is a mental state, one has to exert efforts to produce this mind and it is of a conceptual nature, there is thought associated with it. There is no need for the practitioner who generates this level of mind to have realized any kind of ultimate nature.

When one attains the path of seeing, the first bhumi, this same mental state of wishing becomes inseparable with the transcendental knowledge of realising emptiness. When one is absorbed in the meditation of realising ultimate emptiness, there is also the sense of bodhicitta within this but not in the form of conceptual thought. In the ordinary person's case, the mind that is focused on emptiness and the mind that is focused on the state of enlightenment (bodhicitta), are distinguishable; they are of a conceptual nature. In the case of a Bodhisattva who is in meditative equipoise, whose mind is focused on the ultimate emptiness, the bodhicitta still remains in his mental continuum inseparable from emptiness and this is regarded as the ultimate bodhicitta.

The bodhicitta that does not realise emptiness is called relative while that which does is called ultimate bodhicitta. There is no difference in the naming of a practitioner who attains the first bhumi, however up to this stage the Bodhisattva can still regress, change the course of his practice, and become a Hinayana practitioner. Remaining a Bodhisattva is not certain until the attainment of the first bhumi when it becomes irreversible. Avalokiteshvara, being an Arya, means that he has already attained the first bhumi. So he is not in the form of an ordinary Bodhisattva, being an Arya Bodhisattva, his understanding is based on the ultimate bodhicitta. For this reason he is titled the *'Mahasattva', 'the Great Minded One'*. As he is the embodiment of compassion, as he has this special emphasis on a particular quality he is also called 'Mahasattva'. He is called an 'Arya', 'a Superior' or 'Noble Being', because he has attained one of the ten bhumis.

The actual teaching is divided into four sections: The first is the question put by Shariputra. The second is the answer given by Avalokiteshvara. The third is the approval by the Buddha. The fourth is the rejoicing by the assembly:

*Then at that time, through the power and blessing of the Buddha, Shariputra asked Avalokiteshvara: "How should a son of lineage train who wishes to practise the profound perfection of wisdom?"*

In other words, how should a beginner practitioner engage in the practise of the perfection of wisdom? 'Son of lineage', which of course implies 'daughter of lineage' as well, refers to the practitioner who has entered the Mahayana fold.

When the order of practise of a sadhana is explained, we usually first detail the lineage. This is followed by the explanation of refuge and compassion. The factor of lineage is the condition of the mental continuum of the practitioner. When it is said that someone is in the lineage of the Buddha, it means that he or she has entered into a path by which his or her mental continuum has become the cause of attaining Buddhahood.

Lineage (*gotra*) can be of different types: for example, the lineage of Buddha, the lineage of a Shravaka Arhat, the lineage of a Pratyekabuddha Arhat. General lineage is explained in the sense of Buddha-nature (Tathagatagarbha), the nature of the Buddha that is in the mental continuum of every sentient being. The mind of every sentient being is clear and pure by nature.

If the minds of sentient beings were by nature deluded, then there would be no method or antidote by which these delusions could be destroyed and then there would be no chance for sentient beings to develop with respect to mental attainment. Something that exists by nature cannot be changed. However, the delusions which arise in the minds of sentient beings are not there by nature, they are not inherently existent. Even from the relative point of view, they are not the nature of the mind. Delusions are usually equated with the sky being clouded over. The clouds are not a permanent aspect of the nature of the sky, they come and they go but the clear aspect of the sky always remains. In the same way, the nature of the mind is clarity, the delusions accompany the mind as long as one remains in samsara but they are subject to destruction as long as the necessary antidotes and methods are applied. The fact that the mind is clear by nature means that one is able to attain the state of Buddhahood.

One's lineage is also determined by direct contact with a particular path of practice. One who has entered into the Hinayana path also, of course, has this clarity of mind, this Buddha-nature, but for the time being, it is not ripe enough or suitable to enter into the Mahayana fold. One will remain in this lineage until one has attained the Hinayana result. After this, as the clarity of mind still remains, one will automatically enter into the Mahayana fold, continue with the practice and the final attainment will be Buddhahood. It is for this reason that the definitive teaching of the Buddha is said to be the vehicle of the Mahayana. The ultimate state of liberation is said to be Buddhahood. Although the attainments of Shravakas and Pratyekabuddhas are states of liberation, they are only on a temporary basis. They are only for those beings who cannot go directly into the Mahayana and attain the highest enlightenment.

When a practitioner enters directly into the Mahayana fold then he is said to have entered into the lineage of the Buddha. When a Bodhisattva attains the first bhumi, he or she is said to have entered into the firm lineage of the Buddha, which means that when he has ascended the different levels of the path, he will definitely attain the state of Buddhahood. With this result, there will be one more Buddha and through this Buddha's teachings, there will be other sentient beings led on to the Mahayana path and then there will be more attainment of Buddhahood. In this way, the lineage of Buddha is preserved unbroken. For this reason, a Bodhisattva who has attained the first bhumi is said to be an upholder of the lineage of the Buddha. But generally, any practitioner can be a son or daughter of lineage, whether on the Hinayana or Mahayana paths, as ultimately he or she is heading for the state of Buddhahood.

As explained earlier, the profound perfection of wisdom refers to the knowledge gained through all three yanas, so lineage is not necessarily to be associated with the mental continuum of a Mahayana practitioner. According to the Yogachara School of thought (Mind Only School, Chittamatra School), lineage is not explained in terms of the ultimate nature of the mind but from the clarity aspect. When it is explained from the Madhyamaka or Middle Way point of view, both clarity and emptiness are incorporated, that is, the mind being clear and empty of any inherent existence, is considered as the seed of Buddhahood, as Buddha lineage.

What is called in other texts the base consciousness (*alaya vijnana*), becomes the causal tantra in the context of the trilogy, cause tantra, path tantra and result tantra. This *alaya vijnana* is also linked with the lineage of the Buddha, or the

Tathagatagarbha, the Buddha-nature. When we are dealing with this base consciousness, the clarity aspect of the mind is more emphasised, whereas when we are dealing with the Tathagatagarbha, the emptiness aspect is more emphasised. Because of possessing the mind that is clear and empty of any inherent existence, one has entered into the general lineage.

As far as the Mahayana lineage is concerned, in addition to the possession of this clear mind, the mind of enlightenment, bodhicitta, is added, which then directly connects one to the state of Buddhahood. So generally, when lineage is explained from the clarity aspect of the mind, any practitioner of the three yanas is a son or daughter of lineage, however, from the Mahayana viewpoint, one who has generated bodhicitta is such a son or daughter of the lineage.

So this covers the initial question asked by Shariputra. The next section is the answer of Avalokiteshvara, which is divided into two parts. Firstly, the answers which are applicable to those disciples with a lower faculty of mind, followed by the answers applicable to those with superior faculties of mind. The first answers are explained in terms of the five paths: the paths of accumulation, application, seeing, meditation and no more learning. The answer that applies to the paths of accumulation and application is given together. This is explained briefly first of all and then more extensively. Briefly then:

*Avalokiteshvara replied to Shariputra, "A son or daughter of lineage who wishes to practise the perfection of wisdom should look at phenomena in this way. They should correctly view the five aggregates as empty of inherent existence.*

This emptiness of the five aggregates should be realised subsequently. This means that, at the time of the path of accumulation and application, the practitioner understands this emptiness only conceptually. However, conceptual understanding can be a valid cognition or it may be an invalid cognition. In the beginning, the practitioner's conceptual understanding of emptiness will not be a valid cognition, because there will be imaginary understanding based on imperfect reasoning. After some time, in the course of practise, there will arise a conceptual understanding of emptiness that is a valid cognition and this is called inferential valid cognition.

In terms of logic terminology, when something is realised or known, as long as the knowing of that thing is non-deceptive, then it is a perfect knowledge. The mind state here is described as valid cognition. In the case of perception, the eye seeing a real visual form is considered as valid perception. What is perceived is a true object, in terms of relative truth, is when there is no deception in terms of the contact between the consciousness and the object. Thus, after the seeing of a particular visual object by the eye, one can make use of this, or go and obtain that particular thing, as this seeing is not deceptive.

If what is seen is not there in actuality, if one is not able to make use of it, for example, if it is false vision, then this type of eye consciousness is considered as an invalid cognition, invalid perception. This is in relation to perception, which knows a thing directly.

There is another type of mind that is conceptual by nature but is also capable of understanding things in a non-deceptive manner. This is also a type of valid cognition known as inferential cognition or subsequent knowledge, as it is not a direct knowledge, such as perception but it knows a particular thing by depending on certain causes. Only when these causes are there does it arise. This is the explanation of what is meant by saying that in the course of these two paths, the emptiness of the five aggregates should be subsequently realised.

This means that there is no direct realisation of the emptiness of the five aggregates when the practitioner is on these first two paths, the only valid understanding at this time being through inferential cognition. This is when the various reasonings mentioned in the Madhyamaka texts are applied in the course of one's meditation practise. So one first studies these reasonings, then contemplates on them and then finally meditates on them. After the accomplishment of meditation there will be a direct perception or knowledge of the object in question. This will come at the time of the path of seeing. All the four paths before the path of no-more learning are paths where the practitioner is engaged in the accumulation of merit. Although there are two types of accumulation, the accumulation of merit and the accumulation of wisdom, the former is more emphasised at the time of the ordinary practitioner, that is, the first two paths, as there is no understanding of the ultimate nature, by which one can accumulate wisdom. This will be more emphasised after one has attained the first bhumi. Only at that time, will there be a direct realisation of emptiness and one's mind becomes transcendental knowledge and one will have a basis on which to accumulate wisdom. The text then states:

*Form is emptiness, emptiness is form, form is not other than emptiness, emptiness is not other than form.*

The aggregate of form is proved to be empty of inherent existence, by the application of the four profundities. Only after the attainment of wisdom can one, through the application of the four profundities to the aggregate of form, then apply this to the other four aggregates:

*So in the same way, feeling, discrimination, compositional factors and consciousness are said to be empty.*

That is, one should apply the same method that one used to establish the aggregate of form as empty of inherent existence, to the other four aggregates. The aggregate of feeling is the mental state in which one has the five different types of sensations: pleasure, suffering, satisfaction, dissatisfaction and neutrality. The difference between the feeling of pleasure and the feeling of happiness or satisfaction is based on them having different causes, namely the sense consciousness and the mind consciousness.

The feeling of pleasure, which is linked to any of the consciousnesses of eye, nose, tongue, ear, or body consciousness, is known as pleasure and is related to the body, whereas the feeling of happiness is related to the mind consciousness. This does not mean that one is an entity of body and the other is a pleasant feeling in the mind. Feeling, in general, is a mental quality or state.

Suffering is also divided into two, based on whether it arises from a sense organ or from the mind. The feeling of neutrality is of a subtle nature, but is only considered as one category. The aggregate of discrimination or perception is another type of mind or mental formation in which the mind 'grasps' the uncommon characteristic of a particular phenomenon. The sense of recognition of a particular thing is called the mental state of discrimination. One 'sees' a thing to be different from other things, a particular characteristic which is not present in other things. Compositional factors or the aggregate of conditioned existence includes all other mental states. Included here are the mental factors of virtuous, non-virtuous and deluded mind. It includes all these mental states and some things that are not mental, which are called associated compositional factors and non-associated compositional factors. The former refers to all types of mental states related to the main mind, while the latter refers to the qualities of certain substances.

There are five kinds of similarities by which a mind and a mental state are considered as associated to each other:

(i)   They 'grasp' the same object
(ii)  They have the same aspect
(iii) They have the same sense organ as support
(iv)  They have the same substance
(v)   They belong to the same time.

An example of a non-associated compositional factor is the characteristics of a compounded phenomenon. A compounded thing is produced, exists and disintegrates, or arises, abides and ceases. It is an impermanent thing, it is subject to change, it definitely has these three aspects of production and it is these qualities of arising, abiding and ceasing that are considered non-associated compositional factors.

The aggregate of consciousness includes the main mind, the main types of awareness. These include the six consciousnesses of eye, ear, nose, tongue, body and mind, according to the lower Buddhist schools of thought, (Vaibhashika and Sautrantika), or the eight consciousnesses, with the addition of base consciousness (*alaya vijnana*) and afflicted consciousness, (*klesha manas vijnana*), according to the higher schools of thought, (Yogachara and Madhyamaka).

The knowledge that is aware of the visual form is called the eye sense consciousness, which is a type of mind that is linked to the eye sense organ. Similarly with the ear consciousness, this is supported by or depends on the ear sense organ. So it is the same up to the body sense consciousness, which depends on the body sense organ to be aware of the object of touch, which is a tangible object.

So these five are called physical consciousnesses, which do not mean they have a physical nature but that they depend on the sense organs that are physical forms. The sixth one, mind consciousness, does not depend on a physical sense organ but has as its support sense organ the former moment of the mind. The previous moment of the mind acts as a support for the next moment of the mind.

Afflicted mind is considered as part of the sixth consciousness, mind consciousness. It is that distinct part of the mind that 'grasps' at the notion of self or the person as a discrete entity. Base consciousness is the ground for these other seven. It is not aligned to any particular object but it serves as a foundation for all these other seven, which do have a particular object as their focus. The visual form is the object of eye consciousness, the tangible object of touch is the object of body consciousness and the notion of 'I' is the object of afflicted consciousness and so on. The base consciousness can be described as the 'clarity' constituent of the other seven minds; it is the subtle form of the other seven.

When it becomes gross or coarse, then it becomes aligned to the different objects and it becomes one of these seven minds or it becomes feeling or perception or a particular mental state as described previously. The five aggregates (*skandhas*), function as a basis on which we impute the 'self' (*atma*), on which we establish the formation of a 'person' (*pudgala*). As the individual parts of the body together function as the basis for the imputation of a 'body' as a collective whole, so do these five aggregates function with respect to imputing a 'self'.

This is one way to establish the emptiness of self (*pudgala nairatmya*), as although the root of all delusion is 'grasping' at a 'self', before this can happen, one must already be grasping at one's own five aggregates as inherently existent. As Arya Nagarjuna said, "As long as there is true grasping of the five aggregates then there will be true grasping to self, resulting in delusions and karma, which lead to the cycle of birth and death."

So the attitude of 'self-cherishing' and 'other' arise as a result of the true grasping to one's own five aggregates. If one does not grasp the five aggregates as inherently existent, then one will know that the person imputed on to these does not inherently exist either. So the same method used to establish the emptiness of form is used to establish the emptiness of the five aggregates.

The aggregate of feeling does not exist inherently either, as it is not produced by any of the four alternatives: i) by itself, ii) by another phenomena, by any cause separate from itself, iii) by a phenomena that is the same, as well as separate from itself, or iv) by some phenomena other than these three alternatives. The thought may arise, if a phenomenon is not produced from any of the four means of production, then how does production through dependent arising come about?

According to Madhyamaka, it is accepted that things are produced depending on causes and conditions. In relative truth all phenomena are accepted as they appear, the result arising from a cause or causes, so dependent origination comes about through cause, condition and result. This is to be distinguished from any of the four alternatives of production, which are used in the course of analysis, as they refer to inherent production or inherent existence, which is the complete opposite of dependent arising.

If one accepts the idea of interdependent origination, then one is rejecting existence through inherent production. Those who accept the latter and reject interdependent origination, cannot, the Madhyamakas argue, establish any form of production, even in relative truth. The Madhyamakas state that inherent production is to be refuted on the grounds of it being illogical. Now, if one denies interdependent origination and inherent production has also been refuted, then there is nothing left in relative truth to accept.

Candrakirti, in the Madhyamakavatara, states that in the other philosophical schools, the establishment of both relative and ultimate truth is false, is imperfect. In terms of relative truth, these schools cannot even establish the existence of appearances, what appears to the worldly mind. In terms of the ultimate truth, they accept something as inherently existent, so they again fail in the establishment of the ultimate viewpoint. Candrakirti likens these proponents of other philosophical schools to one who, while climbing a tree, has let go of one branch but has been unable to grasp another, so there is nothing to prevent one from falling down. If one retains one's grip while grasping the next branch, one can continue to climb, but if one loses both grips, one will definitely fall.

If one cannot establish the relative truth and one cannot establish the ultimate truth, then one has failed in establishing both levels of truth. As there is no correct foundation, then there can be no realisation. To say that on the relative level, that a thing is not produced by any of the four alternatives and to say that it arises as a result of interdependent origination, is the same thing. The philosophical tenet that accepts emptiness, accepts all phenomena in the relative truth, whereas those who deny emptiness must also find any form of acceptance of the existence of phenomena untenable, as the foundation is not there.

If inherent existence is supported, there is no possibility of accepting phenomena as they appear; there is no possibility of establishing interdependent origination. So the same reasonings are applied to prove the aggregate of feeling as empty of inherent existence. Feeling is emptiness, emptiness is feeling, feeling is not other than emptiness, emptiness is not other than feeling. This is the application of the four profundities to the aggregate of feeling, and then this is applied to the other aggregates of discrimination, compositional factors and consciousness.

The mind that understands this fact, whether it is either the understanding of emptiness on the ultimate level or the understanding of dependent arising on the relative level, is in the practitioner, it comes under the aggregate of consciousness. However, when it comes to establishing this mind as being empty of inherent existence, then one is referring to this very mind which analyses, which understands. One still retains this mind. It exists through dependent arising. One can have a mind that appears. The mind that arises through interdependent origination and the mind that is established as empty of inherent existence come to the same thing. It is for this reason that emptiness is said to be form.

Emptiness is not separate from form; emptiness is form. The knowledge of the inseparability of dependent arising and emptiness is brought in the context of understanding the ultimate nature of phenomena. If the understanding of emptiness is not related to dependent arising, to the appearance of phenomena, then this understanding will become one-sided; it will be aligned to the extreme of negation - nihilism. One is only negating something, there is nothing accepted.

There are two types of negation mentioned in the logic texts, mere negation and negation with affirmation. The former means there is nothing asserted after negating the postulate, whereas the latter means that after the negation, something is asserted as valid in its place. For example, compare the negation of a pot abiding in space and the negation of a pot on the table. In the case of the state of non-existence of the pot in space, then there is only the negation of the pot. There is no other thing one can accept after the negation of the pot; there is nothing else one can grasp at. In the case of the state of non-existence of the pot on the table, then there is a thing accepted after the negation, the table. The table is the same as the negation of the pot. When there is no pot on the table, it is a table free from 'pot', empty of 'pot'.

So there is the emptiness of 'pot' but there is something one can accept, which is the table. If one merely negates all appearances and does not accept anything with regards to this emptiness, this is an extreme viewpoint and is to be abandoned. This is not the case here, as one accepts dependent arising. Only when one has the theory of dependent arising, can one safely put forward the theory of emptiness. These two are dependent on each other. Because something is empty of inherent existence, it is dependent arising, because something is dependent arising, it can be established as emptiness.

So this is the meaning of the first two profundities, form is emptiness and emptiness is form. The third and fourth profundities are, form is not other than emptiness and emptiness is not other than form. This means that form and emptiness are not separate entities, like a table and a chair in conventional truth. They are of the same essence or nature, the emptiness being the ultimate nature of a phenomena and its form is the apparent aspect of that nature. To the worldly mind, it appears as a form, to the awakened mind, it is understood or 'seen' to be empty of inherent existence.

Seeing its form is said to be seeing the conventional, relative truth, seeing it empty of any inherent existence is said to be seeing its ultimate nature, the ultimate truth. This is the profundity of the two truths as one entity. This also explains the fourth profundity of different aspects - that it is of one base or essence but has two different aspects. Two different characteristics are seen in the form of the two truths. To the worldly, deluded mind, a particular phenomenon is seen as a form but not as emptiness. One aspect is known or understood but not the other, which is the ultimate nature.

To the awakened mind, a phenomenon is seen to be empty of any inherent existence, its ultimate nature but the conventional truth, the appearance aspect is not seen.

It is because of the ultimate nature that conventional truth can be established. This is the profundity of ultimate truth. Because of dependent arising in relative truth, the ultimate truth of emptiness can be established. This is the profundity of relative, conventional truth. The profundity of two different aspects is explained in terms of these two being established on the one essence of phenomena but appearing to two different minds.

It is easy to say form is emptiness but it is difficult to contemplate on and it is much more difficult to meditate on. It is very, very difficult to have a direct realisation of the fact that form is emptiness. In order to be able to meditate in this way, it is first necessary that one has contemplated on this. In order to be able to do this, one has to first have a definite understanding, hence, the need to rely on the different reasonings. This brings us to the four main reasonings of Madhyamaka. These are used to establish phenomena as empty of inherent production. In order to prove form as empty of inherent existence, one has to know that it is empty of inherent production and that it is empty of inherent cessation. Before one can prove that it is empty of inherent cessation, one must first establish that it is empty of inherent production. Form is not considered to be inherently existent, as it is not produced through any of the four alternatives, which are as we have already stated:

i) By itself
ii) By another phenomenon, by any cause separate from itself
iii) By a phenomena that is the same, as well as separate from itself
iv) By some phenomenon other than these three alternatives

It is not necessary for every practitioner, every analyst, to think on all the four alternatives. As long as one has no doubt that a phenomena is not produced by itself, the first alternative, then it is not necessary to go through all of them. However, there are some ideologies that purport that a thing can be produced by itself. There are some philosophical schools that believe that the cause and result are of the same nature; that the cause remains in the form of the result. Only the outer appearance changes and the inner nature remains the same. So when a result is produced by the cause, it is produced by itself, so they argue.

This is negated when it is said that a thing is not produced by itself. If this were possible then there would be continuous production of this phenomenon, there would be no chance of the production of other results. There would also be no need for this one phenomenon to produce itself again, as the purpose of production is to exist, to produce. Once it exists then there is no purpose in it being produced again. By these reasonings, one can dispel any doubts connected with the production of a phenomenon by itself.

The general doubt one encounters, however, is in regards to the production of a phenomenon by a separate cause. In the case of form, one may think that a form is produced by a cause that is separate from itself. For example, one could propose that smoke is caused by fire, which is separate from the smoke. As it is the inherent existence of the phenomena of form that one is attempting to establish here, which means there must be inherent production of form, then if one accepts that it is produced by a cause separate from itself, this means that one is accepting that form is inherently produced by a cause inherently separate from the result, the form. The cause and the result being separate is based on their inherent nature. This would mean that they are completely separate from each other, leaving no possibility for any kind of relationship between the cause and result.

When one accepts anything as inherent, as true, as substantially existent, then it is always on the basis of something that is not dependent but something which arises by itself. This would mean that the result being separate from the cause is the same as the result being separate from any other individual phenomena. For example, in the case of a corn sprout. If one says that it is produced by the corn seed which is inherently separate from it, that it is produced by a cause that is inherently separate from it, then the corn sprout being separate from the corn seed is the same as the corn sprout being separate from, say a rice seed.

Conventionally, the rice seed is seen as a cause of a rice sprout, but not a corn sprout. But if one accepts that the result and the cause are inherently separate, then there would be no difference in the nature of a phenomenon being separate from any other thing. If this is accepted, then the person who exists today and the same person who exists tomorrow, are inherently separate and this would be the same as today's person being inherently separate from any other person.

So, whatever faults there are in another separate entity, will come up in this state of being separate. If a result is produced by a cause inherently separate from it, then there is no reason why that result is not produced by all the phenomena in the world that are separate from it. There would be no difference in being inherently separate. So this reasoning is used in the philosophical analysis. It is not the same as what we accept as separate in the relative context because relatively what we accept as separate is on the basis of interdependence. South being separate from north is only on the basis of these two depending on each other. However, if one considers south to exist by its own inherent nature, then there is no need to depend on north. So even though there is no north, one still has this south, which is not possible.

This analysis is used in relation to the production of phenomena. In this way, one will come to the conclusion that form is not produced by a cause that is inherently separate from it. Now for the third alternative: As long as there is no production from a separate cause or production from a cause which is the same as it, then naturally a phenomenon can not be established as being produced by a cause which is both the same and separate from it.

The fourth alternative is, 'produced by a cause that is neither the same nor separate from it', which means production of a result without a cause. This is impossible to accept. This would mean that there would not be any effort needed in the relative, conventional sense to produce a result and that there would not be any relationship between cause and result. This would mean that there would be no need for practise to achieve a spiritual result, realisation because things arise by themselves, not through causes.

Through this line of reasoning, one can come to the conclusion that phenomena are not produced without causes. Other than these four means of production, there is no other way that a phenomena can be produced inherently, the fifth alternative, so one can conclude that it is not produced inherently. When it is not produced inherently, then there is no way one can prove it exists inherently. So this leads to the understanding of the non-existence of this particular phenomenon, which means one will see it as empty of inherent existence.

In this way, form is established as empty of inherent existence. This method of establishing the emptiness of form can be contemplated in the mind again and again, so the conceptual image will, in the beginning, become clearer and clearer. Then one can advance to the next practise, which is meditating on this. Focusing more one-pointedly, as one has already examined it through analysis, by contemplation. So slowly, one's understanding will improve conceptually as a result of which, one can achieve the path of seeing, when there will be a direct realisation of that particular phenomenon, which one has proved to be empty of inherent existence.

*Question:* How does form arise?

*Answer:* Do you mean the existence of form in the relative truth? The arising of form is established in the relative truth through dependence, the theory of dependent arising, through cause, condition and result. The knowing of a form is dependent on one's mind. Depending on one's mind the form is seen. The apparent existence of the form is dependent on its cause and condition. There is no further analysis of whether that cause is the same as or separate from the form. It arises by depending on the mind that sees it.

*Question:* If the person today is not the same as the person tomorrow, how can one accumulate karma?

*Answer:* We accumulate karma in the relative truth. The two persons mentioned in the analysis of whether they are separate or one is used when we are trying to establish the emptiness of person in the ultimate truth. If one accepts that these two persons are separate by their inherent nature, that they are completely separate, then there will be no difference between the difference of the same person at a different time and the difference between other persons, because this separateness is considered inherent. In the relative truth, we do not accept that it is different but we accept that tomorrow's person depends on today's person. Through this dependence there is a link formed. Tomorrow's person is dependent on today's person but it is not similarly dependent on another person, therefore the difference is there, in the relative context.

Through the analysis of the emptiness of the five aggregates, one will then be able to progress to the establishment of the emptiness of self or person. So *dharma nairatmya* is the emptiness of phenomena or the emptiness of the five aggregates and *pudgala nairatmya* is the emptiness of the person or self. The emptiness of the five aggregates, that needs to be established in order to know the emptiness of self, is only with regards to one's own five aggregates.

If one follows the process of the generation of these graspings, first comes the grasping of one's own five aggregates as truly existent, then comes the grasping of self. Then the grasping of possessions of this self, those phenomena that are related to the self and then there will be the grasping of those phenomena not related to the self, separate from the self, which one considers as 'other' from oneself. This will be followed by the grasping of all other phenomena as truly existent, since when there is the grasping of the self as truly existent, which depends on the belief in the inherent existence of one's own five aggregates, then as one is aware of the five aggregates of other people one will 'grasp at' the true existence of other people. So, all other beings will be grasped as truly existent.

This is also applicable to the outer external phenomena. As far as external phenomena are concerned, the aggregates related to mind are not applicable, as inanimate objects do not have mind and mental states. The aggregate of form is present and the aggregate of non-associated compositional factors can also be present. The example given is the characteristic of a compounded thing. The other three aggregates are not present in inanimate objects.

All the types of delusions arise as the result of grasping one's own as well as others' five aggregates as inherently existent, which then leads to grasping of other external phenomena as truly existent. For example, if one does not have true grasping to the inherent existence of a house, then the house as an object will not become a cause for the generation of different types of delusions in the mind, such as hatred or attachment. So the reason such inanimate objects as a house can lead to such delusions is due to this true grasping of the said house as inherently existent.

When the emptiness of one's own five aggregates and one's own self has been established, then gradually the same method is used to establish the emptiness of other phenomena too. One should keep in mind that the one who is asking the question here, Shariputra, is a Hinayana realiser, whereas the one who is giving the answer is a Mahayana practitioner, Avalokiteshvara. Generally, this teaching of emptiness is not meant for a Hinayana practitioner. Of course, it is meant for Shariputra, as he is already a Hinayana Arhat and there is no other attainment in the Hinayana vehicle higher than Arhatship. So Shariputra will not be aspiring to any other Hinayana result, the only state of realisation he would be aspiring to acquire is the Mahayana state of highest enlightenment, or Buddhahood.

According to the Madhyamaka system, when a certain practitioner reaches the highest level of the Hinayana, which means one has become an Arhat, then that is the ultimate attainment of this path. When one has completed this path, then one will naturally see the benefit to be accrued by joining the Mahayana level and it is in this context that Shariputra is being taught. So Shariputra will join the Mahayana fold from the beginning of the first path, the path of accumulation. There are other philosophical viewpoints within the Madhyamaka system that assert that after Arhatship is attained and the Mahayana fold is entered, then one will enter from the path of seeing. According to another viewpoint, one will enter from the path of meditation, as an eighth bhumi Bodhisattva.

Generally, however, it is accepted that no matter how realised a Hinayana practitioner may be, since one still lacks many of the qualities of a Bodhisattva, whether it is the transcendental knowledge of understanding emptiness or the practices of method such as compassion and bodhicitta, one has to enter at the beginning of the Mahayana path, which is the path of accumulation. So it is said that there can be two types of practitioners on the path of accumulation, one who has realised emptiness directly and one who has not. There is a difference of opinion as to whether someone who is not an Arya is capable of realising emptiness directly or not.

If one goes through the Mahayana path gradually, then during the paths of accumulation and application one does not have a direct realisation of emptiness. However, if one attains the state of Arhatship and then joins the Mahayana path of accumulation, this practitioner has a direct realisation of emptiness that is called fundamental knowledge, as mentioned earlier. This incorporates the knowledge of the emptiness of self and one's own five aggregates.

After joining the Mahayana path of accumulation, this knowledge will not cease, it will still continue. The fact that all types of knowledge and qualities will continue as one becomes more advanced on the path is applicable to all situations. As one traverses the different levels of the path, the forms of faults and delusions will become less and less but the positive qualities of mind will increase more and more. When we talk about the three vows of the Pratimoksha, Bodhisattva and Vajrayana, then some would argue that the vows are taken in this order. First of all one will take the Pratimoksha vow, after that when one takes the Bodhisattva vow, one becomes a Bodhisattva. However, the nature of these vows is not that distinct, they are not to be understood in terms of having physical forms.

This has to do with the mind that makes the resolve to refrain from certain faults and activities that are contrary to that particular practice. According to some, when one takes the Bodhisattva vow then the Pratimoksha vow is no longer there. It is transformed into the Bodhisattva vow and when one receives the Vajrayana vow then the Bodhisattva vow is no longer there, as it is transformed into the Vajrayana vow. Finally, one will only have the Vajrayana vow. However, this is not acceptable, as the good qualities in the mind always increase, which means that the vows will be added to each other. So after one has taken the Bodhisattva vow, one is endowed with two vows, then when one takes the Vajrayana vow, one is endowed with three vows.

The Vajrayana practitioner is called the 'one with three vows' - the Pratimoksha, Bodhisattva and Vajrayana vows. This indicates that all the qualities will increase, whether one is on the path of accumulation or the path of application and the attributes one acquires on the later paths will be added to these. At the time of final attainment one will only have positive attributes and no faults. The practitioner who has attained Arhatship and joins the path of accumulation has a direct realisation of emptiness whilst remaining in meditative equipoise. On other occasions, one still has a conceptual understanding of emptiness, as one has not realised the emptiness of all phenomena, from all aspects, the emptiness free from all extremes of conceptual elaboration.

When it comes to realising emptiness in these other contexts, at this stage, the practitioner still has to use conceptual understanding. This will only be transformed into direct realisation when one has attained the first bhumi, the path of seeing, in the Mahayana. So these differences occur with regards to the different levels of practitioners entering the same path.

With regards to explaining the emptiness of the five aggregates to a Mahayana practitioner, in the context of the first two paths, where one does not have a direct realisation, one has to engage in the study and contemplation of the emptiness of all phenomena. So the emptiness of the five aggregates is mentioned here so one can then apply this method to the emptiness of self and then to the emptiness of all phenomena. On the path of seeing, in the Mahayana, the realisation of emptiness is not limited to one's own five aggregates or the self, it pervades all phenomena, internal as well as external. As this direct realisation of emptiness pervades all phenomena, then that which precedes it, which is the study, contemplation and conceptual meditation of it, should also be in the form of establishing all phenomena as empty of inherent existence. We have been dealing with the answer given by Avalokiteshvara based on the first two paths.

Avalokiteshvara then continues his answer in the context of the path of seeing:

*In this way Shariputra, all phenomena are empty, that is, without characteristic, there is no production, no cessation, they are neither stained nor stainless, undiminished or increased.*

Previously, with regards the first two paths, we were able to establish the emptiness of phenomena through the four profundities, now here, phenomena are established as being empty through being free from the eight types of conceptual elaboration or eight extremes. Firstly, when it says that phenomena are empty, it is in terms of their nature. Secondly, with regard to that, all phenomena are without characteristics. 'That which functions', is considered as the definition of a compounded thing. It is possible that a compounded thing is empty of inherent existence but still some characteristics may exist. So it is also necessary to prove that the characteristic of a certain thing is also empty of inherent existence. All phenomena are therefore said to be without characteristics, without any uncommon characteristic by which a phenomena is differentiated from another. This also refers to what is called self-characteristic and general characteristic. Self-characteristic refers to the uncommon qualities of a certain thing, while general characteristic refers to the qualities of a thing that are also prevalent in other phenomena. The quality of holding water is the function of a vase or a pot. This can be said to be the self-characteristic of this vase or pot. If it is compared to the function of a pillar, the pillar is also a compounded thing which has a functional activity but it does not function as a vase, so the form of function of a vase is the vase's own characteristic. That which is produced and subject to change is a characteristic of the vase and also of the pillar, so this can be considered as a general characteristic of the vase. So both these types of characteristic do not have any inherent existence.

Phenomena are also not produced by any of the four alternatives, as mentioned earlier, and there is no cessation. Cessation refers to inherent cessation. This method of establishing all phenomena as having no inherent cessation is used in the context of the relationship of cause and result with regards to karma. When the Yogachara School asserts that in order to link the action and the result, it is necessary to establish a substantial entity that will do this, they use the idea of base consciousness (*alaya vijnana*). They say that this continues, it always remains throughout samsara, even after an action is performed and there is no evidence of the action left, still it will continue until it is ripened, until the result arises. There is no action that continues but the result of the action will definitely arise. The base consciousness acts as a link between the cause and the result. Even after many lifetimes, one can still establish the fact that something is the result of an action performed in the distant past. The Sautrantika School accepts the mind consciousness as the basis to establish this link, instead of the base consciousness (*alaya vijnana*).

The Vaibhashika School asserts that there is a substance known as acquisition or attainment (*prapti*). After one performs an action, then the action comes to an end but that action leaves behind another substance, which is called the acquisition. One has acquired the imprint of the action. Of course, an imprint is left on the mind but it is not this imprint that links but the other substance that has arisen after the cessation of the action, the acquisition. This is established on the basis of mind but it is not considered to be a mental state.

The Madhyamaka refutation of all these substances is that there is no need of such a substance to link the cause and the result, because the cause has not ceased inherently. This is the meaning of the text saying there is no cessation. It looks to the worldly mind that after an action is performed then it has ceased completely but actually, it has ceased completely only in the relative sense. The same logic is applicable to production as well. When something is produced, it is through dependent arising, which means it is produced in the relative sense; there is no inherent production.

Whoever accepts a thing as inherently existent falls into the extreme of nihilism, this happens in the case of schools of thought who believe that an action ceases inherently. As they have accepted the action as inherently existent at the time of the performance of the action, then when the action ceases they think it has ceased inherently. Then there is a fear that it has become completely extinct and then the search for a link arises but in the case of the Madhyamaka reasoning, this is not necessary.

The text then goes on to say that all phenomena are stainless, without any stain of delusion. As mentioned earlier, in the ultimate truth, the mind is by nature clear; it is not always accompanied by delusions. The delusions are only temporary or adventitious, which means that they can be separated from the mind. It is not like fire and the heat from that fire, where the heat is always inseparable from the fire itself. We say that heat is the nature of fire. If one places a metal poker in the fire then when it becomes very heated up it looks as though it becomes ember-like, a part of the fire but when the heat source is removed then the poker will return to it's own nature of being metallic, which is not of the nature of heat.

In the same way, the mind is not of the nature of all these delusions, so there are methods by which these delusions can be destroyed, leaving the mind without them. The text continues to state that all phenomena are also not stainless. Even though one may have this understanding of the mind as being without stain or delusions, if there is a phenomenon that is grasped as inherently existent that is without stain, this is still a false notion. The fact of being stainless is not an ultimate thing.

The text then continues with, 'all phenomena are without increase or decrease'; they are neither diminished nor increased in any way, in the context of the state of the ultimate truth. In the relative sense there are certain things that increase and there are certain things that decrease but with respect to the ultimate nature of all phenomena, emptiness, nothing will increase or decrease as a result of being realised or spoken of by a Buddha. In another context, we also say that the ultimate nature of all phenomena is not made by anyone, that all phenomena are empty of inherent existence is not a fact that started with the teaching of the Buddha. It is not that before the arrival of Buddhist teachings that things existed inherently but after the Buddha proclaimed emptiness then everything became empty of inherent existence. If this were so then the ultimate nature would become a produced one, something that was dependent on a 'doer'; someone who performs an action. This means that it would be subject to further changes. Patently, this is not so, which is why it is said that there is no increase. Even after the realisation by an enlightened mind, the emptiness of phenomena remains the same.

Some philosophical schools state that not everything is empty of inherent existence, that there are some things that do exist. Just due to these philosophical ideas, the nature of emptiness will not turn into something that exists inherently. If it did then the emptiness would decrease, so this is the meaning of saying that there is also no decrease in the nature of all phenomena. The ultimate nature of all phenomena is realised directly by the transcendental knowledge of the practitioner on the path of seeing, through knowing it to be free from all these eight extremes of conceptual elaboration. So this understanding will be complete, from every aspect. During the first two paths, the realisation of emptiness is through the knowledge gained by study, contemplation and meditation in a conceptual way. After the fourth level of the path of application, the practitioner attains what is called 'supreme dharma' (the dharma of all the most excellent but still deluded qualities in samsara). In the next moment, one will attain the path of seeing, which is the first generation of an undeluded dharma or quality. All these paths apply to the knowledge of the practitioner; it is not some kind of external stage. At the time of the path of seeing, a direct knowledge of emptiness is attained and this knowledge is undeluded, as one has also got rid of all the delusions which cause rebirth in samsara. All qualities before that may be of different levels of understanding but they are still considered to be mixed with delusions, so are labelled deluded knowledge.

*Question:* How does memory function between different lifetimes?

*Answer:* It is explained in terms of the link or relationship between karma and result. It also follows the same rule that is the causes are in one life and the results are in the next. Memory is usually considered to be a result of knowledge. When one knows something then one will remember that later. In this case the knowledge becomes the cause and the memory becomes the result. Or forgetfulness, actually, the mental state of forgetfulness is also considered as memory in the Abhidharma, as it's negative aspect or opposite. It comes under the same category of mental state.

*Question:* Where is the memory stored between different lifetimes, given the nature of the continual flux of cause and effect, what is it that remembers and where does memory come from?

*Answer:* We have one consciousness that is called store consciousness, *alaya vijnana*, so naturally that is where everything is stored. It is not only the memory that one has the problem of storing but all the karmas that we are performing have to have a place to be stored. According to the Madhyamaka view, one must know the relationship between cause and result. At this stage the only thing we can do is to explain it in a conceptual way. As one understands more, in the practical sense, then one will know oneself. The idea of 'between lifetimes' can be understood by applying how one knows and remembers things in this very lifetime.

*Question:* I thought there might have been a biological basis for memory. Western science thinks that there is part of the brain that functions as memory, a physical reality.

*Answer:* Not the mind, so when you die that comes to an end so there is no memory, is that what you are referring to? As far as I understand, science explains everything from what we see, not only memory but the whole mind and the mental states. Rebirth is also in this category. This is from another context, from a different outlook. The only thing I can say is that this is not acceptable from a Madhyamaka philosophical stance. Some form of connection may have been found between the cell and memory but it is not this thing that is the only cause that produces memory. It is related, of course. Our mind is also related to our body. The next moment of the mind is dependent on the previous moment, as a cause but the body functions as a condition.

*Question:* Can memory be in the body, stored in the cells and stored in the consciousness separately?

*Answer:* According to Madhyamaka philosophy, memory is a mental state, which is a type of mind, coming under the category of the aggregate of compositional factors (*samskara*). All types of mental states are included in this aggregate. There are certain sorts of mental states that may arise as mental formations of sense consciousness. For example, there may be a memory that is related to the eye consciousness. The eye consciousness is in turn related to the eye sense organ, which is a physical thing, so, on that level it can be connected but memory itself is a mental state. As far as memory in the next lifetime is concerned, it differs with the quality of the mind. Not only with regards to memory but also in terms of the characteristics of a particular birth, there are different levels of mind. Science may say that there are different levels of body structure but then these have their own causes. The whole body structure is also a result of the karma formed on the mind. Since there is a difference in the nature of karma that was formed, then there is also a difference in the memory or any other quality in the next birth, for example, some people may have some memory of past lives, some may not and some people may have a particular mental quality, some may not. Some may have a very continual memory of past lives and some may have only an occasional memory of past lives. These things are related to the nature of the cause, the nature of the karma that one has performed.

*Question:* With regards to the aggregate of feeling (*vedana*), why is there only one category of neutrality or indifference, where there can be positive and negative feeling, or attraction and aversion, with regards to the body and with regards to the mind? Experientially, it would seem to me to be quite different to become neutral or indifferent to feelings with regards to the body and to feelings with regards to the mind, and as such quite a useful distinction.

*Answer:* We can make this distinction. However it is not usually made, as the classifications are made on an ordinary, relative level. The feeling of indifference (equanimity, Skt: *upeksha*, Tibetan: *gtang snyoms*), is rare, in any moment, in the majority of sentient beings. Either it is dissatisfaction, suffering or suffering in the form of what we usually call pleasure which as it is subject to change will turn into suffering at some later moment. The feeling of indifference is only to be found in the higher levels of existence. It is rare and it is to be understood as being implied in the positive and negative feelings.

*Question:* Is the capacity to be indifferent, to have equanimity, developed simultaneously with regards to the feelings of the body and mind?

*Answer:* It is developed on equal terms, there is no gradual process that first one succeeds with regards to the body and then later with regards to the mind. With regards to the word *gtang snyoms*, the word is translated into English as both indifference and equanimity. If one thinks that it has the meaning of being equal, that both the feeling of aversion and attraction are present in equal amount, then this is the wrong interpretation. It means a feeling that is neither pleasant nor unpleasant. It is one term that the Tibetans use for different meanings. There is a definition for each particular usage. By the word alone we cannot be sure, as it can be used to signify other things as well. So we can use the word equanimity, by giving a definition of this then it will work. It is a mental state and every mental state is aware of something, aware of at least itself. It is not aware of unpleasantness because there is no unpleasantness present.

*Question:* If a person thinks that something is unpleasant, I am aware of it but I am going to feel indifferent?

*Answer:* That is a different thing. If there is a second mind that is aware, then that is a different mind. That is not this feeling of equanimity that we are talking about. In order to define this we don't have to make use of another thing.

*Question:* In what order should one pursue the points you mentioned to break down the grasping at the five aggregates as being 'real'?

*Answer:* No general order is mentioned. As long as one has not established the understanding of the self as completely empty of inherent existence then the other methods can only act as some sort of temporary panacea.

*Question:* But that is a very hard technique to work on, the self as being empty?

*Answer:* Yes, a very hard one but it is more effective. Once one has negated that then all one's possessions will naturally disappear.

*Question:* What are the signs of the first bhumi?

*Answer:* Some of the signs mentioned in the texts are that the Bodhisattva on the first bhumi always remains in a very happy mood, very joyful. So the title of this bhumi is 'The Very Joyful Bhumi'. One now knows that one has attained the path of seeing, one has gone beyond samsara and one has come quite close to the attainment of Buddhahood. One has also become more capable of benefiting sentient beings, so at this stage, one becomes very happy. Another sign is that one is very accomplished in the perfection of giving (*dana paramita*). If an occasion arises when one has to give even the parts of one's body, then there is no hesitation and there is even respect to the recipient of this act of giving. If you see someone like this, then you should call all of us and together we will pay homage!

With regards to the different paths which deal with the destruction of negativities, whether it is the path of seeing or the path of meditation, two stages are always present, the first stage of directly dealing with the negativities and the next stage of actually becoming free from that negativity.

The first stage is called the uninterrupted path while the second stage is called the released or liberated path. So these two stages of each one of the five paths are not to be considered as separate from them. These five paths are general for every practitioner but within these five there are different levels. As soon as the practitioner realises emptiness directly as a result of the path of application, one is said to have acquired the path of seeing. At this moment however, one has not necessarily become completely free from delusions which cause rebirth in samsara. So there is a stage when the transcendental knowledge of realising emptiness and delusions may co-exist.

In the general case, it is not necessarily so that when two things are opposite then one of them will destroy the other one. Depending on circumstances, both can destroy each other. In the case of fire and water, the tangible object of heat and the tangible object of cold, these two are considered as non-simultaneous opposites. These entities remain in the relative truth on a certain basis but hot and cold do not remain simultaneously, so they are considered as opposites. When the tangible object of heat is of a greater degree then it will destroy the existence of it's opposite, the tangible object of cold and vice versa, of course.

Now it is not so in the case of grasping of inherent existence and the transcendental knowledge of emptiness. One may think that the same reasoning may be applied, as the knowledge of emptiness is an opposite force to this grasping of inherent existence, so it should be able to destroy it and consequently, why could not the grasping at inherent existence destroy the transcendental knowledge of emptiness?

It is not just that they are opposites. One of these two, the grasping of inherent existence, is contrary to the actual mode of being of reality, with the nature of reality. One of the objects of these two mental states conforms to the mode of being of the entity in question. It is because of this that one can eliminate the other one. The grasping at inherent existence has as an object something that is not true, which does not remain after logical analysis, whereas the knowledge of emptiness has the state of emptiness as its object that remains even after analysis. One object will be established after analysis and one will not, because one of them is not the actual state of being of that phenomenon. Due to having the support of the mode of being of that phenomenon, then the knowledge of emptiness will destroy the grasping of inherent existence, but not vice-versa.

At the time of the path of seeing, when the knowledge of realising emptiness arises, then the first stage is said to be in the process of the destruction of this grasping. This does not mean that there are two conceptual thoughts or two different minds manifesting at the same time. The first generation of the path of seeing is said to be not yet freed from the grasping of inherent existence. This does not mean that when one has generated this knowledge of emptiness one still has the grasping of inherent existence. When the mind is focussed on emptiness directly, one cannot have simultaneous grasping at inherent existence. However, the imprint or seed of that grasping is still there in the mind of the practitioner, so one is said to have still not got rid of the grasping. In the next moment, that seed of the grasping is destroyed and as a result of this there won't be any re-emergence of this grasping. There won't be any conceptual thoughts that grasp inherent existence. Of course, there are still some residues of these imprints but these are not considered to be grasping at inherent existence. They become another form of negativity that also has to be abandoned; these will be abandoned at the time of the path of meditation.

So the differentiation between the Bodhisattvas on the path of application and on the path of seeing with regards to the destruction of negativities, is that the former has only destroyed the gross part of these negativities but not their seed, while the latter has eliminated the very root of these negativities, as a result of which, there won't be any further arising of these delusions. The condition of the practitioner on the path of application is likened to cutting only the upper branches of a tree, which will eliminate the existence of this tree for some time but due to the root not having been eliminated, it will still grow.

The condition of the practitioner on the path of seeing is likened to the severing of the root of the tree; as a result of this there won't be any further growth of these delusions. While a practitioner is engaged in the practice of acquiring the knowledge of understanding emptiness, he gradually trains and the knowledge becomes finer and finer until it becomes omniscient knowledge. This degree of improvement is based on the clarity of the understanding of emptiness as well as the destruction of the delusions. In the case of the path of seeing, the knowledge of that Bodhisattva directly realises emptiness and in this respect there is no difference in the knowledge of the path of seeing and the knowledge of the path of meditation. At the time of the path of seeing, one has got rid of only one section of the delusions, the objects of relinquishment, whereas the practitioner at the time of the path of meditation has eliminated more of the main negativities, as a result of which one's knowledge of realising emptiness has become more advanced, finer in quality.

As one ascends these levels of the paths, one will eliminate more and more negativities. One will naturally want to know what these objects of relinquishment are. It was mentioned earlier that with respect to the first two paths, the root of rebirth in samsara is the grasping of inherent existence. This has the two aspects of grasping of self as inherently existent and the grasping of phenomena as inherently existent. As a result of these two kinds of grasping, there will be delusions and uncontrolled rebirth in samsara. The delusions of ignorance, hatred and desire, which cause uncontrolled rebirth, are the objects of relinquishment of the path of seeing. As mentioned previously, there are two categories of objects of relinquishment, those relinquished through seeing and those relinquished through meditation. All the delusions that have been destroyed by the path of seeing are considered as the objects of relinquishment through seeing. There are still other negativities that the Bodhisattva has not destroyed and these have to be destroyed in the course of the path of meditation. These are called the objects relinquished through meditation.

During the first two paths, the practitioner destroys certain negativities and these can come under either of the two categories. The object relinquished through seeing does not mean that this occurs exclusively at the time of the path of seeing. It is called this because the root, or seed, of this type of object of relinquishment is destroyed at the time of the path of seeing. Similarly, the root of the objects of relinquishment through meditation is only destroyed at the time of the path of meditation but certain of these types of the objects of relinquishment will have been eradicated earlier. The next section is the answer based on the path of meditation. The text says:

*Therefore, Shariputra, because of this, emptiness has no form, no feeling, no discrimination, no compositional factors, no consciousness, it has no eye, no ear, no nose, no tongue, no body, no mind, no form, no sound, no smell, no taste, no tangible object, no phenomenon. It has no eye element up to no mind element.*

*It has no element of eye consciousness up to no element of mind consciousness. It has no ignorance, it has no cessation of ignorance, it has no ageing and death, it has no cessation of ageing and death.*

*It has no suffering, no origin of suffering, no cessation, no path, no transcendental knowledge, no attainment, no non-attainment.*

To recapitulate, at the time of the first two paths, the Bodhisattva should engage in the practise of understanding the emptiness of the five aggregates. Other than these five aggregates, there are no other phenomena that one has to establish as empty of inherent existence. At this stage, the understanding of emptiness is taught through study, contemplation and conceptual meditation. At the time of the path of seeing, this has become a direct understanding. This is followed by the path of meditation that is divided into the following two categories. The worldly path of meditation and the undeluded path of meditation, sometimes called the uncontaminated path of meditation. The worldly path of meditation comprises all those practices of meditation that are not connected with, which do not need the understanding of emptiness. There are different types of practice of meditation that are not aligned with the realisation of emptiness, for example, the four formless absorptions and the ten pervasive absorptions. These are considered as worldly practices of meditation. These can be used as methods to overcome certain delusions at particular levels of worldly existence. For example, when someone engages in the practise of the first level of absorption, the meditation of gross and subtle aspects, this is a meditation where one will focus on the faults of the desire realm and through this one sees the benefits of the first level of dhyana. The purpose of this meditation is to get rid of some negativity. The method it pursues is that there exists something relatively better that is used as an objective in order to destroy the negativity of the lower level. One may come to know the faults and sufferings of this desire realm but not necessarily be able to see the faults of the form realm, which is a higher level in worldly existence but is still contained within samsara. So the mind is focussed on the faults of the desire realm and the benefits and advantages of the first dhyana of the form realm. When one has become accomplished in this meditation, then one will have got rid of the delusions in the desire realm. As a result of this, one will be reborn in the first level of the form realm.

However, because the method utilising the knowledge realising emptiness was not used, the delusions of the desire realm were not destroyed from the root, as a result of this the being in the form realm may again generate the delusions of the desire realm and once again take rebirth in the desire realm. It is for this reason that the rebirths in the three realms of existence, the desire, form and formless realms (*kama, rupa* and *arupa dhatu*), ascend and descend according to circumstances. If one is reborn in a very high worldly existence, where one has got rid of many of the faults of other types of worldly existences, such as a being born in the formless realm, then all sorts of pleasant and unpleasant feelings have been eradicated. This being is on the level of attaining some sort of spiritual realisation, which may appear to be similar to the attainments of the different paths. However, it is not so, because the method used to arrive at this result was also the worldly method of the gross and subtle aspects, so the root of the delusions was not destroyed and as a result of this the mind still possesses the imprint of those delusions. It is only a matter of other conditions arising for the delusions to reappear. Even if one has reached the pinnacle of worldly existence, the fourth dhyana of the formless realm, where one has eliminated the gross aspects of the delusions of all other worldly existences, this does not mean that the delusions will not come back again. This contaminated, worldly method of meditation is not powerful enough to destroy the root of the delusions, so one could still possibly take rebirth in a very low worldly existence in the desire realm.

The type of meditation that is referred to in the text that we are dealing with here, is a result of the path of seeing and is definitely an uncontaminated or undeluded meditation, it is not of a worldly nature. It is quite different from the meditation experienced by a being in the form realm. It is for this reason that the object of meditation is studied closely. One has to be very careful what one is meditating on. Having a clear power of the mind remaining in one-pointed meditation is not enough in the case of a practitioner wishing to achieve the state of liberation.

There is another worldly meditation of the form realm called the absorption of non-consciousness, where the meditator is able to stop the arising of all the gross forms of consciousness, feeling and discrimination and it is like one is remaining in an unconscious state, without any mental formations. However, even this method is still not strong enough to destroy the root of all the delusions, that is the grasping of the self as inherently existent.

All beings in the form and formless realms are considered as god-beings. Devas exist in the desire realm also. Above the world of normal human beings, there are six different levels in the desire realm where all the beings are devas, starting with the realm of devas of the four directions, the devas of the Thirty-third realm up to the devas who dwell in Tushita heaven. In the fourth level of the form realm, there is one realm of existence, where devas throughout their entire life remain in this absorption of non-consciousness. This does not mean this god-being is completely without a mind. He still possesses a mind but the mind does not function in the way the minds of beings in the desire realm function, with the development of many gross mental formations. The life-span of devas is said to be much, much longer than the life-span in the desire realm.

However, there is still a gross mind at the time of birth and at the time of death but other than the consciousness of birth and the consciousness of death, throughout their lifetime there is no development of other gross types of mind. These devas are also referred to as 'long-life gods', which is considered as an inopportune birth when we talk about the difficulty of obtaining the precious human rebirth. The human body is said to be endowed with the possibility of eighteen pre-requisites - eight opportune states and ten endowments.

Rebirth in one of the three lower realms, the hell, hungry ghost or animal realms are considered as inopportune states. Also mentioned as inopportune is rebirth as a long-life god, as there is no opportunity in that life for engaging in Dharma practice. So the level of this long-life god is much higher than an ordinary human being but with respect to engaging in Dharma practice, it is the human birth that is considered more fortunate. Any attainment of these absorptions is not helpful or beneficial as far as destroying the delusions of worldly existence.

The path of meditation lasts for a long time as, in the case of the Mahayana, it extends from the second to the tenth bhumi. A Bodhisattva on the first bhumi has acquired the knowledge of the path of seeing. As explained earlier, the paths refer to the different knowledge acquired at different levels. The knowledge of realising emptiness of the Bodhisattva on the second bhumi is considered as the path of meditation. This knowledge is no longer in the form of conceptual meditation, like that of ordinary practitioners. It is said that it is difficult to differentiate between the contemplation and meditation of an ordinary practitioner. It is also said that the mind of one in the desire realm has not attained the actual level of the mind of meditation.

What we call meditating is actually a form of contemplation, thinking. This means that the mind does not stay one-pointedly on a certain object. However we try to place the mind on one object, it still wanders to the different aspects of that object, so this becomes the practise of contemplation, of thinking, which is a precursor to meditation. Within this contemplation, the form that has less distractions and conceptual thoughts is considered as a form of meditation. When the ordinary practitioner meditates, it is usually the conceptual form, whether it is an analytical or one-pointed meditation. It does not become just awareness without any conceptual thought, like for example, eye consciousness. This does not happen until one attains the path of seeing.

In the path of meditation, it is not a case of thinking upon the object of the path of seeing in a conceptual way, which is one type of meditation. In the path of seeing, the direct knowledge of emptiness has arisen for the first time; prior to this, the understanding was only conceptual. So this knowledge is not of a new class, it belongs to the same class of undeluded knowledge, which began at the time of the path of seeing. From then on, whenever the mind of the practitioner is focussed on emptiness, it will be an undeluded realisation.

So the knowledge of emptiness of the path of meditation is in the same form as at the time of the path of seeing, it seems to be a repetition of the previous understanding. However, it is not accepted that it is focussed on the same object. Since the object of the knowledge is the state of emptiness, this emptiness cannot be understood from the point of view of a permanent or impermanent entity or substance. As long as it is free from these permanent or impermanent factors, we do not say that the emptiness that is the object at the time of the path of seeing still remains at the time of the path of meditation. This is not acceptable.

The understanding of emptiness at the time of the path of seeing is through direct realisation. That same mode of understanding is maintained at the time of the path of meditation. This is continued right through the path of meditation until the state of enlightenment, until Buddhahood. The first contact of a visual form with eye consciousness can be likened to the path of seeing. The subsequent moments of the eye consciousness looking at this same visual form can be likened to the path of meditation. If we explain things from the point of view of momentary consciousness, the first eye consciousness that sees the visual form and the subsequent moments that see the same visual form are of course not the same substance. Every moment is a different eye consciousness and with respect to the object, every moment it is a different object. The eye consciousness of the tenth moment is not looking at the visual form that was seen by the eye consciousness of the first moment. However, due to the continuity of the eye consciousness, the later eye consciousnesses become brighter or clearer. There is a clearer view of the visual form. Even though it is a different object seen in the later moments, there is an increase in the clarity aspect of the object. Similarly, in the case of the path of meditation, the knowledge of the Bodhisattva does not remain the same, it is a changing knowledge but due to the continuity of the nature of looking at emptiness, the direct realisation of emptiness becomes clearer and finer, until it reaches the ultimate state where there is no need for further habituation with or meditation on this object of emptiness. After the path of seeing until the path of no-more learning is considered the path of meditation. The text states, 'Emptiness has no form, no feeling, no discrimination, no compositional factors, no consciousness.'

At the time of the path of meditation, the Bodhisattva realises emptiness without any inherent existence of the five aggregates. The difference between now and at the time of the first two paths is that it is direct, not conceptual.

The text continues, 'It has no eye, no ear, no nose, no tongue, no body, no mind' - up to it has no phenomena. This is referring to the emptiness of the six organs and the six objects, the twelve sources or *ayatanas* in Sanskrit. One classification of phenomena is made on the basis of the five aggregates. Another one is made on the basis of the twelve sources, while a third classification is made on the basis of the eighteen elements, or *dhatu* in Sanskrit.

There are two types of *ayatanas*, the inner *ayatana* and the outer *ayatanas*, the inner sources and the outer sources. The inner sources include the six sense powers or organs, which are the eye, ear, nose, tongue, body and mind sense organ, *indriya* in Sanskrit, which can be translated as power. So this means that in the emptiness that the Bodhisattva on the path of meditation realises there is no eye sense organ. Neither is there the eye consciousness, nor the eyeball that sees the visual form. It is the eye sense power, the energy that enables one to produce sight, which functions as the dominant cause of the act of seeing. In order to produce eye consciousness three conditions are necessary:

(i) The condition of object
(ii) The condition of sense power
(iii) The condition of consciousness.

When phenomena are classified into twelve sources, only the first two of these three conditions are mentioned. In the text when it says that there is no eye it does not refer to the eye consciousness that sees the visual form. It refers to the emptiness of the eye sense power that causes the eye consciousness. In the same way from ear up to body consciousness three conditions are also necessary. In the case of body consciousness we need a tangible object such as the element of earth, which is the object of touch. Then we need the body sense power, which is within the body, it is the not the body we see but is considered as a type of form, which is not visible to the eye consciousness, it is not a mental state. Then we need the consciousness, which is the immediate moment of consciousness prior to the one in question. So, with regards to eye consciousness, these three conditions have to be present in the first moment. The visual form which functions as an object, the eye sense power which functions as a dominant cause of producing this eye consciousness and the prior moment of consciousness to this eye consciousness. When one awakens from sleep and one sees a visual form for the first time on this particular day, which means that there is no eye consciousness prior to that, there is still a consciousness that functions as an immediate cause to the generation of this eye consciousness and that is the mind consciousness, the sixth consciousness. One has this whether one is asleep or awake.

The condition of object is considered as the outer source, the condition of sense power is considered as the inner source. Both are sources of the production of consciousness. So this explanation of the inner source being what is referred to here in the text also applies from ear up to mind sense power. There is mention of the mind sense power which functions as a dominant condition to produce the mind or sixth consciousness. Eye up to body consciousness are called the five physical sense consciousnesses and these are dependent on a form as their dominant condition. The mind sense power does not depend on a form; it is dependent on the preceding moment of consciousness.

These six sense powers function as conditions from within the mental continuum, from within the body of a person, so they are considered inner sources. The external objects such as visual form up to the tangible object are considered as outer sources as they also function as conditions for the production of these consciousnesses but from the outside. The sixth object, which is called the object of phenomena (*dharma ayatana*), is not necessarily an external object, as it encompasses all things that are not the objects of the first five consciousnesses. The mind consciousness can focus on all phenomena whether they are mental, animate or inanimate, of the past, present or the future; compounded or uncompounded. The object of mind consciousness means the object of all thought.

The emptiness that the Bodhisattva on the path of meditation realises is not only free from the five aggregates but also free from the twelve sources, the six inner and six outer. From the point of view of an immediate understanding of emptiness there is no need to mention all these phenomena. However, doubt may arise as to whether it is practical to see the emptiness of all phenomena or only of certain things and not of all things. These differences arise at the time of the practice on the Hinayana level, where the realisation of emptiness becomes limited to certain phenomena. As far as the Mahayana level is concerned, the manner of realising emptiness on the path of seeing is the same as that realised at the time of the path of meditation. The Bodhisattva at the time of the path of seeing will realise the emptiness of all phenomena. So it is to establish that the emptiness of all phenomena is realised by these Bodhisattvas that the explanation is from the point of view of the emptiness of the five aggregates, the twelve sources and the eighteen elements. So Avalokiteshvara is teaching that the Bodhisattva on the path of meditation realises emptiness directly and this emptiness pervades all phenomena.

*Question:* You said that the initial experiences of emptiness are still tainted by some residues of the delusions. How do they manifest?

*Answer:* The immediate purpose of attaining knowledge is to go beyond samsara, to get rid of the sufferings of samsara. But even this state beyond samsara is not necessarily the ultimate state. The Hinayana realiser has also gone beyond samsara, they have none of the sufferings of samsara but they still have what is called undeluded ignorance. There is still some ignorance that obstructs the way to achieving omniscient knowledge. There are still many things that they do not know, although they do not have any delusions of a samsaric nature. There are still impure appearances, which are not grasped as inherently existent but there are other levels of grasping and the obscuration of knowable objects. These are the faults in the mind that are of a subtle nature. These come under the category of the object of relinquishment through meditation and will be gradually eliminated in the course of the path of meditation from the second to the tenth bhumis.

*Question:* If I see this visual form and then I go to touch it, is my eye consciousness the previous consciousness that acts as a dominant cause for the touch consciousness?

*Answer:* No, we don't say that. Whenever there is not an immediately preceding consciousness of the same nature, then it is always the mind consciousness that functions as the prior consciousness. There can be a relationship formed between the body consciousness and the eye consciousness that was immediately preceding it but it is not in the context of that eye consciousness functioning as an immediate condition for the body consciousness.

*Question:* So there are still the three conditions for mind sense power, as the last moment of mind consciousness acts as the dominant condition?

*Answer:* Yes. Its immediate condition and its dominant condition are the same.

*Question:* Can the visual object, which is the object of eye consciousness, be an object of mind consciousness?

*Answer:* The visual object can also be an object of mind consciousness but it is not exactly the same visual object. It is the general visual object. This imagined form of the visual object can still be said to be an object of the mind. The mode of grasping the object by these two consciousnesses is different, one is direct and the other is conceptual.

*Question:* I can accept that one cannot have two conceptual thoughts simultaneously but are you saying you cannot have the bodily consciousnesses together, say hearing and seeing?

*Answer:* No. Of course one may have these simultaneously. When one is looking at something, experiencing eye consciousness, it doesn't mean that one is deaf at that time. These different consciousnesses can arise simultaneously.

*Question:* So one can have all six going at the same time?

*Answer:* Yes. That is what we have generally.

*Question:* How would you distinguish between analytical and discursive thought?

*Answer:* By analytical thought, I mean the mind that analyses, investigates a certain point. Discursive thought rests upon that certain thing; remains focussed on that certain thing, for example, the impermanence of samsara. There are many ways to prove that samsara is impermanent, so one thinks upon these various reasonings and then tries to come to a conclusion. This is analytical thought. The mind is working on impermanence in an analytical way. After coming to a conclusion one may just think that samsara is impermanent, the mind focussing on one particular thing, this is discursive thought. This is how the two are usually described in terms of the practitioner's meditation. Analytical mind, when it is referred to in the process of the practice of meditation, is that which examines. Not all types of mind that are wondering about a particular phenomenon are considered analytical. They may be looking at many different aspects of that phenomenon but analysis is only a part of practice after which one-pointedness becomes possible. Mind that wanders and becomes a distraction, an obstacle in the course of meditation, is not considered as analytical.

*Question:* Is it better to use sense organ or sense power as a translation of the Sanskrit term *indriya*?

*Answer:* I think sense organ is fine for the five physical organs but sense power is better for the sixth one of mind. But as I have already said, sense power is closer to the meaning of the Sanskrit word *indriya* and the Tibetan word *wang po*. *Indriya* can be said to come from the word *Indra*, the Hindu deity of power, the one who is in charge, the king, the lord. So these are in charge of the function of seeing, hearing and so forth. So power is better, I think.

*Question:* One cannot really attain meditation until one is on the path of meditation, should what we call meditation be called contemplation?

*Answer:* Do you mean that what we call meditation is not actually meditation? Yes. Of course we don't want to remain in the desire realm forever, which is what we mean here. The purpose is to go higher. When one goes higher there will be a mental state where there will be real meditation. In the case of a human being, one can produce the mind of the form realm. One can engage in the practice of the absorption of the form realm, this is not the mind of the desire realm. The body is of the desire realm but the mind can be of the form realm and on that basis one can have meditation. The desire realm mind is very coarse; it cannot function as a support for meditation. With the mind of the desire realm, one-pointed concentration will not become perfect, though we may try on the basis of the ordinary mind of the desire realm. One-pointedness cannot be perfected unless one relies on the mind of *dhyana*, or mind of absorption that only starts in the form realm. The coarse mind, which has a very diverse nature with many thoughts, is the mind of the desire realm but it is on this basis that one begins to work on the one-pointedness meditation.

The text now brings us to the topic of the eighteen elements; the word in Sanskrit is *dhatu*. That which holds something, or functions in its own characteristic way, is usually defined as an element, a dhatu (*kham* in Tibetan). In the case of eye sense power, it is also called the source of eye sense power, the element of eye sense power. It is called the source of eye sense power because it functions as a source to produce a consciousness.

It is called an element of eye sense power because being a compounded entity it has its own special characteristic. It not only produces consciousness, but it can also be a cause of the next moment of eye sense power.

Its own characteristic is the definitional element. It is from different aspects of the same entity that it is given different names or explained in different contexts. So it is also called a source and an element. The twelve elements of the sense power and their objects are the same as the twelve sources. The difference in labelling is explained here from the point of view of having its own characteristic. The six elements of consciousness are the result of the first twelve elements. The six elements, which are the objects of consciousness and the six sense powers will function as causes, as a result of which we get the six consciousnesses.

These consciousnesses, the eye, ear, nose, tongue, body and mind consciousness, are also compounded entities which also have their own characteristics, so they are also called elements. They are also called the element of eye sense consciousness, to the element of mind sense consciousness. However, regarding the practice on the path of the meditation on emptiness, there is no element of any type that is grasped by the practitioner. The emptiness which one realises is free from the inherent existence of all these eighteen elements.

The text goes on to state that, 'in this emptiness, there is no ignorance, no exhaustion of ignorance. No ageing and death, no exhaustion of ageing and death.' The main knowledge of the practitioners on these different levels relates to meditative equipoise. During the meditation session, it is the direct realisation of emptiness. So throughout these explanations of the five paths, it is explained from the point of view of realising emptiness. While this sutra deals with the different aspects of knowledge of the five paths, explicitly telling us about the realisation of emptiness, the way it is explained through the realisation of the emptiness of the five aggregates, of the twelve sources and the eighteen elements, also tells us about the relative aspect, of the things which the practitioners must realise as emptiness.

So not only the emptiness aspect (*shunyata*), not only the aspect of the wisdom (*prajna*), is explained, but the method aspect (*upaya*), is also taught at the same time. As in every teaching of the Buddha, there is only a difference of emphasis, of stress, whether the ultimate is more stressed, or the relative truth is. The Buddha's teachings consist of explanations in an explicit and implicit way, of both the ultimate and relative truth. When the teachings of the Buddha are classified into the two categories of definitive and non-definitive or teaching that requires interpretation, the definitive teaching is the one that explicitly explains or deals with the ultimate truth but implicitly it also teaches relative truth, the method aspect.

This Heart Sutra and also the other sutras of the Perfection of Wisdom, explicitly deal with emptiness, the ultimate truth that is emptiness. But implicitly, as explained earlier, they deal with the different levels of understanding. In the case of different levels of knowledge, these are not only on the basis of understanding emptiness but they also differ with respect to the method aspect of practice. Now the method aspect of practice is based on the relative truth. In order to engage in the practice of the method aspect, one has to know the different aspects of the relative truth. For that one has to know about such things as the relationship of cause, condition and result, the system of the birth and death in samsara, how a person with the five aggregates functions and how one relates to this with respect to different lifetimes.

So all these will have to be studied and understood, in order to understand the method aspect of practice. While it is explicitly mentioned here that the Bodhisattva on the path of meditation will realise the emptiness of the five aggregates, the twelve sources and the eighteen elements, at the same time the things which are to be negated, which must be seen as empty of inherent existence, are also explained, for example, the twelve sources. We also know that a self or person is imputed on the collection of these twelve sources and eighteen elements. In other words, a being consists of these different qualities, or elements.

Through such explanations, one will come to know about the activity or functioning with respect to an eye and a visual form, so these are explained side by side with the explanation of emptiness. Now when, in the text it is said that in emptiness 'there is no ignorance, no end of ignorance up to no old age and death', it is referring to the emptiness of the twelve links of interdependent origination, or as it is called in many translations, 'the twelve limbs of dependent arising'. The Tibetan word is in fact a limb or a branch. But it can also mean a link that is formed between different stages.

There are twelve links by which the system of birth and death in samsara is explained, by which a sentient being is bound in the cycle of birth and death. The Bodhisattva on the path of meditation will realise emptiness but after coming out of the meditative session, it is not that the Bodhisattva is going to teach his followers nothing but emptiness. One will also have to teach the method aspect, the relative aspect of phenomena. When it comes to the explanation of how a sentient being is bound or takes rebirth in this way, how one travels through the cycle of birth and death, then the explanation of the twelve links of dependent arising will come.

The first link of dependent arising is referred to when it says in the text, 'there is no ignorance.' So one should first of all be familiar with the twelve links of dependent arising, they are the link of ignorance, the link of compositional karma (or compositional action), the link of consciousness, the link of name and form, the link of sources (the ayatanas), the link of contact, the link of feeling, the link of craving, the link of grasping, the link of existence, the link of birth, the link of ageing and death.

So the first link is the link of ignorance (*avidya*) and the last is the link of ageing and death (*jara-marana*). In the text, the first and last are mentioned, the other links are thereby implied. Now the link of ignorance is the same as self-grasping, the grasping to inherent existence. All the faults and delusions of samsara depend on this root cause, self-grasping. This grasping of the self as inherently existent is called here the link of ignorance. Due to the grasping of an inherent self, the mind is not aware of the actual nature of the 'self', which is empty. So it is called ignorant. However, while it is named the link of ignorance, it is not only the mental state of ignorance one is talking about, in the course of different lifetimes, not only ignorance exists, there are other forms of delusions which arise, which exist at the same time as ignorance, these also have to be understood on that level but the main contributing factor is ignorance.

After this, because of ignorance and other delusions, action is created. One performs an action; this is called the link of compositional action (*samskara*). Within this, virtuous action, non-virtuous action and unshakeable action are contained. Unshakeable action refers to action in the form and formless realms (*rupa dhatu and arupa dhatu*). Virtuous and non-virtuous action refers to the two types of action in the desire realm (*kama dhatu*). The third one is the link of consciousness (*vijnana*). When a child is born, the first consciousness, which is the result of previous action and which is the cause of all the other links in this lifetime, is called the link of consciousness. Now the word 'link' is used because it joins the first and the following link. The link of consciousness can mean only the mind consciousness, as in the beginning, at the instant of birth, there will not be eye, ear, nose, tongue and body consciousness. So it is the first consciousness of a child, the mind consciousness. After that we have the link of name and form (*nama rupa*), which means the five aggregates. There is also a form at the time of the arising of consciousness but it is not in a gross manner such as to include all the five aggregates. After a certain time, as form develops, then it will become the five aggregates. This aggregate of name and form thus also refers to the other four aggregates - the aggregate of feeling, perception, conditioned existence and consciousness.

Now consciousness was already there in the beginning when birth took place but all of the five aggregates only occur concurrently, when the other aggregates are there, so together they become one group, this is what the link of name and form (*nama rupa*) refers to. It is not a form, not a type of form. After that we have the link of sources (*sadayatana*), which refers to the eye source, the eye sense power, up to the mind sense power. Even before that there will be the body sense power because at the time of the formation of five aggregates, there is the body. But there will be a stage when there is a body without the sense organs. Only when the eye, ear, nose, tongue, body and mind sense organs occur concurrently, is it categorised into the one group of the six sources. At that level the being will have all the six sense powers, from eye up to mind sense power. This last category refers to the same mind that was there in the beginning but it was not functioning as a condition for producing phenomena in the gross manner as it does now, so this is why the mind sense power is established again at this stage as a separate category.

Next these six ayatanas will come in contact with the external objects such as visual form, object of taste, smell, touch, hearing and the internal object of mind, as a result of which a mental state will be formed in the mind, which is called 'the link of contact' (*sparsha*). This is also a part of mind, one of the many mental states. Then there will be 'the link of feeling' (*vedana*). Now through the interrelationship of the three conditions, the sense power, the object and the perceiving consciousness, there will be the mental formation in the mind called 'contact', as a result of which one has pleasant, unpleasant and neutral feelings in the mind. So this is called 'the link of feeling' Next, as long as one has pleasant and unpleasant feelings, then there is a mental state that craves or desires to have pleasant and not to have unpleasant feelings. This stage in the mind is called 'the link of craving', (*trishna*). Then comes 'the link of grasping' (*upadana*), which is in fact a sort of stronger type of craving. The first desire you have for achieving pleasant feelings is called 'craving', whereas the mental state by which you actually engage in an activity for achieving that pleasant feeling is called 'grasping'. It is named 'grasping' because it is a mental state in which one is engaged in efforts with respect to external things to achieve pleasant feelings. So this type of mind is labelled 'grasping'. Then we have 'the link of existence' (*bhava*). 'Existence' referring to the mental action formed. After craving you have the mental state of grasping, after which one will actually perform an action. This stage of mind is where the action is formed in the mind and this is called 'existence'. In fact, it is the same as what was mentioned in the second link as 'compositional action' (*samskara*). Usually, the twelve links of dependent origination (*pratityasamutpada*), are explained on the basis of three lifetimes, that is, we complete one cycle of these twelve links of dependent arising in three lifetimes.

So from the link of consciousness to the link of existence, these eight links refer to this present lifetime. In the next life we have two links, the link of birth with the link of old age and death. 'The link of birth' refers to the first formation of the next life and 'the link of ageing and death' refers to the duration of the state of life after birth up to the occurrence of death. In the previous lifetime there were the two links of ignorance and compositional action. This means that in the first lifetime, the previous one, one establishes the two links of ignorance and compositional action; it does not mean that in the first lifetime there are no other links, such as the link of feeling or link of craving because obviously within one lifetime these links of dependent arising are there. However, in the context of explaining one cycle of the twelve links of dependent arising, these two links are explained in terms of arising in the previous life, to show that the links of ignorance and compositional factors already exist. In the present life, when the eight links are explained, then the first two links of ignorance and compositional action are also included, whereas in relation to the two links of birth with ageing and death, then all the former ten links are included.

This method of explanation is to clarify the different levels or stages of one birth, of one lifetime, for example, the link of birth (*jati*) and the link of ageing and death, being relegated to the future life. One should be aware that these two links also include all other former links, namely the link of ignorance to the link of existence. Without the link of ignorance, sentient beings will not generate the different delusions and as a result then they would not perform any kind of virtuous or non-virtuous action. However, it is obvious that sentient beings are still in the process of performing all these actions, these actions which are motivated by delusions, which are in turn motivated or created by the root of the delusions, which is ignorance, so one can see that the other links are there.

Now these twelve links of dependent arising are also categorised into three sub-sections: The sub-section of delusion, the sub-section of action and the sub-section of birth or result. The sub-section of delusion includes three links, the link of ignorance in the first life and the links of craving and grasping in the present life. These three are forms of delusion. When the links of craving and grasping are referred to, these include all the other types of delusion as well. The second sub-section of action includes two links, the link of compositional action and the link of existence. These are both based on the performance of a virtuous or non-virtuous action by a sentient being. In the third sub-section of birth are included the other seven links from the link of consciousness to the link of ageing and death. In the present life the link of consciousness up to the link of feeling, these five links come under this sub-section of result and in the next lifetime we have the link of birth and the link of ageing and death. With reference to these twelve links of dependent arising, two types of action are mentioned, the link of compositional action (*samskara*) and the link of existence (*bhava*). It is explained on the basis of a single sentient being which continues through the link of the compositional factors, to the link of existence.

The nature of the action, however, is divided or explained in two ways. The one form of action or karma that gives the main result, by which a sentient being is projected into a life form, is called the projecting action. For example, an action by which one will be born as a human being or as a god being. The other type of action is the one that completes the formation of that result and is called the accomplishing action, or the actualising action. For example, there are other characteristics or qualities needed for a particular birth. In the case of a human birth, with respect to a life span, it can be short or long, having all the sense organs intact or having defective sense organs. All these different characteristics contribute to the nature of the life of a sentient being. So the projecting action will give the main result and the accomplishing action will determine the different characteristics of that life.

The link of compositional action refers to the projecting action, which determines the main birth, whereas the next action, which is the link of existence, only adds or determines the different characteristics. The second action is still on the basis of the first, it is not a different action, which will give a different birth but in addition to this first action, the other characteristics are determined. To give an external example, with relation to cause and result, it is considered that there is one cause that gives the main result and there are other causes that will assist in making a difference in the nature of the result. With regards to a plant, the seed is the main cause, the projecting cause and the action that will give the main result. Now, whether the result, a crop, is of a good quality or of inferior quality depends on other conditions, such as water, manure and so forth.

These conditions are also causes of the result but are known as assisting causes. They are not the main cause. They are the same as what are mentioned here as actualising action or accomplishing action. The types of delusions, the link of ignorance at the beginning and the links of craving and grasping in the middle are also explained in two ways. The link of ignorance is the main delusion that is the main motivation of the action, the projecting action. Craving and grasping are those delusions that motivate the other types of action, they are called actualising actions.

We can look at these types of delusions from the aspect of motivation. In one particular action there can be two types of motivations. One is the deluded motivation, which is the original motivation or the initial motivation and there can be others that are called simultaneous motivations. Before an action is performed, there is a mental state which functions as a motivation, as a cause for that particular action. Now when you do the actual action, at the same time there is still a motivation or mental state, which is linked to that action. It is not necessary that the simultaneous motivation should be in the same line with the initial motivation. It can differ also.

Due to these differences the action may have different results. In the case of the virtuous action of prostration, if the initial motivation is virtuous, let us say, out of motivation of faith and the simultaneous motivation i.e. the mental state while performing the action of prostration, is also faith, then both motivations are virtuous, then the result will definitely be a virtuous result and the result of happiness. However, if the initial motivation is of a virtuous nature but the simultaneous motivation is not, like disrespect or doubt, then the result of the virtuous action will become smaller. So since one action can depend on these two levels of different motivation, in the same way the cause of birth, which is an action, also depends on different levels of motivation. These motivations are all delusions but they occur on different levels.

A third way of explaining the twelve links of dependent arising is in connection with samsara and nirvana. In the text it says that there is 'no ignorance, no end of ignorance up to no old age and death'. This line shows the entire process of birth and death in samsara. It also shows the method of going beyond this, of obtaining the freedom for oneself from the cycle of birth and death.

Dependent arising is of two types, the dependent arising of deluded nature and the dependent arising of complete purification. The dependent arising of deluded nature is to contemplate on the twelve links of dependent arising in their sequential order as well as their reverse order. To contemplate the twelve links of dependent arising in their sequential order involves looking at the first root in samsara being the root of ignorance and from ignorance compositional action arises, then from it the next link, up to from the link of existence, then the link of birth arises, and as a result of that the link of ageing and death arises. When one looks upon the twelve links of dependent arising in this way, then you will start to understand the meaning of them being linked together, being interdependent.

When one looks at the dependent arising of ageing and death, when one examines or analyses it, one will come to know that is has arisen from birth and that birth in turn depends on existence, it depends on grasping and finally it depends on the link of ignorance. By this method one will come to know the root cause of samsara. So through these two practices of contemplating on the twelve links of dependent arising in their sequential order and in their reverse order, one will come to know the cause and the result of samsara. This way of looking at the twelve links of dependent arising is called 'the dependent arising of deluded nature'.

The other way of looking at it, with respect to nirvana, with respect to complete purification, is to reason that if the link of ignorance is destroyed, is eliminated, then the next link of compositional factors will be abandoned. If this is abandoned then the next link of consciousness will be abandoned. So finally one comes to the elimination of the link of ageing and death. By this method of reasoning, one will come to know the result aspect of nirvana because one will realise that if the former links of dependent arising are eliminated then one will get rid of the suffering of ageing and death.

In terms of the four noble truths, this result aspect of nirvana is referred to as the truth of cessation. So the truth of cessation is the cessation of the sufferings of samsara, the truth that is the exhaustion of the sufferings of samsara. One will then realise that if the first causes or links are destroyed then one will attain the truth of cessation, one will understand the result aspect of nirvana. If one now looks upon the cessation or exhaustion of the twelve links of dependent arising, in their reverse order, which means that the exhaustion of ageing and death depend on the cessation or exhaustion of birth, then one will know that the exhaustion of birth depends in turn on the exhaustion of existence. In this way one will finally come to the exhaustion or cessation of the first link, which is ignorance. Then one will also come to know that this exhaustion of ignorance and its cessation, in turn depends on its antidote, which is the direct knowledge of realising emptiness, the knowledge of selflessness or the knowledge of emptiness. If one gains this, then one will be able to destroy the link of ignorance, which means there will be a cessation of ignorance and in turn there will be a cessation of all the other links. So this reverse order of the twelve links of dependent arising with respect to looking at the cessation or negation will help one to know the cause or path of nirvana.

This way of analysing the twelve links of dependent arising is in the context of nirvana, of complete purification. This is what is being referred to when it says in the text, 'there is no ignorance, no end of ignorance up to no old age and death'. It is not only that the emptiness is mentioned. In order to know emptiness, you have to know the path, the way or the method by which one can understand this and for that one has to know the state of existence or samsara from which one has to liberate oneself. This is understood when one contemplates the twelve links of dependent arising in their sequential and reverse order with respect to the two approaches of deluded nature and complete purification.

On the points which we dealt with yesterday, we will now have a short visualisation of these in the form of meditation so that it will become a little practical, not entirely theoretical. So while I speak, visualise these meanings I describe to you for a while. In reply to Shariputra's question, Avalokiteshvara first dealt with the subject of the emptiness of the five aggregates at the time of the first two paths, so visualise the emptiness of the five aggregates, beginning with the emptiness of the aggregate of form. Reason that emptiness is the aggregate of form and the form is the emptiness, which means the form itself, is the state of emptiness.

The ultimate nature of the form is the emptiness, empty of the inherent existence of the form. There is no other emptiness besides that very appearance of the form, which means that the same form which appears to the worldly mind as a form is understood as empty of inherent existence by the knowledge of an Arya, by the knowledge and understanding of ultimate emptiness. In the course of these two points, place one's mind on the fact that the aggregate of form is empty of inherent existence. In the same way now let us apply the same method to the other four aggregates, thinking that in the same way as the aggregate of form, the ultimate nature of the other four aggregates, of feeling, of discrimination, of compositional factors, of consciousness, are also empty of inherent existence.

Reason that, if one imputes or accepts the inherent existence of these aggregates, then one cannot explain the different activities of these aggregates in the relative truth because one will not be able to explain these on the basis of dependent arising. But since these are not inherently existent, one can accept them as dependent arising and on the basis of dependent arising one can establish the relative truth. So, the other four aggregates are empty of inherent existence in ultimate truth, but at the same time they are dependent arising or they appear by depending on causes and conditions. The fact that these other four aggregates are empty of inherent existence but that they are a result of dependent arising comes to the same meaning.

Next, one's understanding of emptiness should be applied to the twelve sources of consciousness. Visualise that the six internal sources, the eye, ear, nose, tongue, body and mind source power, are also empty of inherent existence. Then the six external sources, source of visual form up to the source of tangible object, as well as the source of the object of phenomena, which is the object of mind consciousness, these six objects of the six consciousnesses are also empty of inherent existence. Not only these twelve sources but also the six consciousnesses which arise in relative truth as a result of them, are empty of any inherent existence.

Visualise in the same way the twelve links of dependent arising as empty of any inherent existence. Although in the relative truth one link arises as a result of another, in the ultimate truth, the Bodhisattva on the path of meditation does not see these twelve links of dependent arising while realising emptiness, so this is the reasoning behind why one should visualise the twelve links of dependent arising from the ignorance to ageing and death as also empty or free from any inherent existence.

*Question:* Could you give us some explanation of the visualisation we just practised?

*Answer:* The phenomena, which are apparent to the worldly mind, are first established as empty. Then, with regards to the four noble truths, there is also the emptiness of cessation, which is usually considered a state of nirvana, the state that the practitioner attains. This is then also established as empty. So emptiness of the different stages is taught as one makes progress along the path.

## 'JOYOUS ELEGANT SPEECH'

*Question:* What do you mean by projecting action and accomplishing action? I think that at some stage Sogyal Rinpoche used a concept of throwing karma and completing karma. Is that similar?

*Answer:* Yes, it is the same. The Tibetan is *'phen byed kyi las* and *rdzogs byed kyi las*. *'Phen byed* is sometimes translated as projecting. The other one is sometimes translated as actualising.

*Question:* Is it the same word as in the word *rdzogs pa chen po?*

*Answer:* Yes, it is the same word but *rdzogs* has two meanings: one is that it has finished; there is nothing left out and another is that it has become full. So *rdzogs chen* may mean that nothingness has become full.

*Question:* If one was following say the Yogachara line of reasoning, the thing that could be carried on the base consciousness (*alaya vijnana*), from one birth to the next, would you say that would be the link of ignorance (*avidya*) and the link of compositional action (*samskara*)?

*Answer:* Yes, we can say *alaya vijnana* would be the support for all this; it would be there continuously. But with regards to the *alaya vijnana,* different stages are mentioned. It will be the one line but at one point ignorance is more obvious and then at the next it is the action. So throughout it is explained on the basis of consciousness. Even when the link of consciousness is referred to, it is not a completely new occurrence of consciousness. There is a consciousness before that, but the link of consciousness is to indicate the consciousness of that life. We do not say the consciousness of one life is a completely new thing because the base consciousness, which continues from the previous lifetime, is still there, is not disconnected.

*Question:* So does the ignorance that carries through have any individual characteristics, or is it just ignorance?

*Answer:* Self-grasping.

*Question:* Is it just the general quality of self-grasping or apart from the karmic imprints can it be stronger or weaker? Does it purify? Does the self-grasping lighten in a sense as people develop?

*Answer:* No. That is not mentioned here. Only that it is the root of all other delusions, which is there in the mind of every sentient being. This aspect of self-grasping is considered as ignorance, in this case, the link of ignorance. Though ignorance can be explained on many different levels, any type of grasping is considered as ignorance because it is the not understanding of the real nature of phenomena. But here it is in the context of self-grasping, because this is the main grasping which creates all other delusions and motivates karma.

*Question:* So in the general sense, at the moment of death, when you die, you will have this subtle self-grasping because you just implied that it came on to the next life?

*Answer:* Yes. You could say that.

*Question:* So after death and through the bardo, (intermediate state, *antarabhava*), is it still there?

*Answer:* Yes, it is still there. Because of this then the afflicted mind (*klesha manas vijnana*) still continues. Otherwise, if it did not continue then there would be a chance of maybe finding a method, a way, for a newborn child to understand selflessness very easily.

In other words, if the imprint or continuity of self-grasping is not there from the earlier life, then one is completely in the 'natural mind'. Then one could be very easily taught selflessness.

*Question:* Is imprint and karma the same thing?

*Answer:* Usually we say the karma leaves an imprint on the mind. Karma is usually explained more in terms of the actual performance of the action. When we prostrate, that is the karma of the body but because of that something is left in the mind, which is the imprint of that karma.

*Question:* Is it actually a Tibetan word you are translating?

*Answer:* *Bag chags*, which means residue.

*Question:* Is this the imprint that *alaya vijnana* is the support for?

*Answer:* Yes, that is *bag chags*. Like a sticker in English. It means that something has stuck there. So in Tibetan *'dod chags* is desire, *nyon mongs* is delusion. Is this a Tibetan lesson?

*Question:* Is *nyon mongs* the same as *klesha* in Sanskrit.

*Answer:* Yes. Some people translate it as defilement but I think delusion is better.

*Question:* If someone has unfortunate mental circumstances, in the mind, is that one's karma? Is it actually one's imprint?

*Answer:* Yes. It is due to your karma. The imprint left by a certain karma is now ripening in the form of this mental disorder. It is the same with any kind of result. What is helpful in this case is, as long as you know it is the result of karma, you will know there is a relationship between a cause and a result. Then the actions that you are going to perform in the future will be more likely to be virtuous, as you now know that they can have a result that you will have to experience. There is also a difference in the way of looking at the result itself. If one knows that it is the result of karma then one will not be depressed or become hopeless. Those who don't know about this cannot directly deal with the problem. If they do not know or cannot explain the situation, then no method to deal with it will be found. If you know the law of cause, condition and result, this theory of karma, then it will work at least to this degree. You will know it is something ripening because of karma and one will do better in future.

*Question:* I was wondering if you could explain a little bit more about grasping and craving. From what I understood, you were saying the second stage grasping is more to do with mental states that involve action. Is that right?

*Answer:* Yes. Craving is the first desire towards achieving better things in life, particularly with respect to the pleasant feelings. Now because you already experience feeling, you know the difference between pleasant and unpleasant feeling. The next moment there is a craving for achievement of experiencing a pleasant feeling, not an unpleasant feeling. That first stage is the craving but you will not stop there. Then there will be a stronger version of that craving, which will then cause you to engage in some action by which you want to achieve the pleasant feeling. The stage of the craving is called grasping when the mind is grasping the objects which will create a pleasant feeling, in your case.

*Question:* I am not quite sure if you are talking about going from link one to link twelve, you said you could either go from ignorance to old age and death, and you could also go backwards from link twelve to link one?

*Answer:* Backwards is only used in the context of practice but it does not happen that way in reality. There are two ways of understanding this order. One is the actual order, meaning when the cause is mentioned first followed by the result then this gives us the actual order, or the substantial order, as it happens in the actual relative truth. Another order is the order with respect to knowledge, which using the example of the four noble truths, we see that the first truth is the truth of suffering, not the truth of the origin of suffering. Now the actual order is that the origin will come first and then the suffering occurs. But here suffering is mentioned first, because with respect to knowing, we will first know the suffering, this is the one with which we have direct contact, next we will be able to find the cause, after that comes the origin of suffering. So this is an example of this order with respect to knowing.

*Question:* In this case does one experience grasping first or craving?

*Answer:* Craving of course, craving and then grasping. It is only in terms of understanding that we can use the reverse order. So the grasping comes from craving and craving comes from feeling. In this way one can understand the relationship of cause and result in samsara, it is in order to facilitate this that these two methods of contemplating the twelve links in this sequential and reverse order are mentioned.

*Question:* If you were practicing, contemplating on karma and what it meant that you were having whatever was happening to you, might not the result of that be that you go from the grasping stage to try to undo that grasping and get to be more aware of the craving as part of practice? Let's say you are caught in grasping, right midstream with actions to try and get something you want and because you are trying to practice, you think: "Ah, let's pause here and contemplate or meditate on this", and then in that process, you actually try and undo the grasping to get back to being in touch with the craving so maybe you can calm your activity. So within practice you attempt to go back.

*Answer:* Yes, you can attempt to go back. You cannot go back completely, of course, unless you have cut off the ignorance. That is what I meant. There are different stages of course. It doesn't mean that in every case, in every sentient being, that these twelve links will come one after another in a very exact order. It is rather a general order that applies to all sentient beings but there are many different circumstances. The grasping may come immediately after craving or the craving may last for a very long time. So it depends on different individuals, especially with regards to practitioners.

*Question:* And both craving and grasping can still really be about valid relative truth, can't they, on a relative level?

*Answer:* Yes.

*Question:* I was thinking there is another level where there is not only craving and grasping in the sense of valid relative truth but that people then get into craving and grasping based on invalid relative truth, that is, not only are they wrong about the origins of happiness on an ultimate level but they are also actually wrong about what will make them happy on a purely relative level. They think they are craving happiness but what they do, the grasping we do, is grasping of things that, even on a relative level aren't those objects because the cognition is actually false. So that is a sort of different level again. But you could have craving and grasping that are at least relatively true?

*Answer:* Yes from the point of view of the mental state, both are the same relative truth. There are two types of minds, mental states which crave and which grasp, these are true in a relative sense. But then of course, it differs if we look from the point of view of getting away from these, then all these, even craving and grasping are false mental states. So in that case then, not only the grasping but also the craving will be avoided. But this does not mean the craving and grasping are not relatively true. They can be, but a cause can operate in the relative truth but after producing a result, the cause is no longer extant, in the relative sense. However, this does not mean that the cause is not relative truth. From the Mahayana point of view there are these levels of the mental state.

*Question:* Do you see the possibility of a gap between feeling and craving?

*Answer:* I think that may be possible. Again it depends on the individual. Just because there is a feeling, one is not necessarily attached to it or craving to attain that. But again it is from this general order that craving will come a moment after experiencing the feeling. So because of having the feeling, then there may be the craving. It is not that as soon as there is the feeling, that there will definitely be a craving immediately after that. That is not the point here.

*Question:* If you didn't fall into craving, you would have to be indifferent to pleasure and pain. Have to not mind which one takes over?

*Answer:* The mind can be in many different mental states, you know. The mind does not necessarily have to be experiencing any feeling, craving or grasping. There are many other mental states through which a sentient being passes. These twelve links are from the point of view of general levels of the sentient being. When we say the link of feeling is present, then at the same time the being also has many other mental states. Like the contact, which was there before feeling, is also there. At the same time the mental state of discrimination, looking at the different characteristics may be present. Or let us say the mental state of awareness. In some cases the mental state of memory is also there. So there are other different mental states through which the person passes.

*Question:* At one stage you mentioned ten mental states that are always present? You did not actually list them for us.

*Answer:* The ten are feeling (*vedana*), perception (*samjna*), intention (*cetana*), contact (*sparsha*), awareness (*manaskara*), interest (*chanda*), determination (*adhimoksha*), mindfulness (*smrti*), concentration (*samadhi*) and wisdom (*prajna*). As far as the practise goes, in order to get rid of suffering, or dissatisfaction, first of all one must come to really know the state of suffering. As the Buddha said at the time of teaching the four noble truths, "The truth of suffering should be understood or known." One may try to get rid of suffering, but one cannot do that by directly dealing with the suffering. Unless the origin or cause of suffering is destroyed, it will not decrease or diminish by itself. In other words, there is no direct method of destroying suffering. One has to know its origin and only by destroying the origin attain the result, which is that the suffering will cease.

It is likened to the treatment of an illness. When someone becomes sick, one cannot directly deal with the sickness. One cannot get rid of it by directly dealing with it; one has to have a treatment that will deal with the cause and as a result of that one can recover from the illness. In the same way the method of getting rid of suffering is to destroy its cause. To demonstrate this next truth the Buddha said that the origin of suffering should be abandoned. What is to be abandoned is the origin of suffering.

Let's look at self-grasping now, with respect to cause and result. Generally, that which is capable of destroying directly is seen to be the cause, as a consequence of which, the result ceases. We have in the mind the mental state of self-grasping, which we know is attached to or focussed on the self. One has to, through logical reasoning establish this self as empty of inherent existence. Now we cannot get rid of the object, the self, directly. It is only by getting rid of the grasping of the object that the object is said to be destroyed or abandoned. This idea is in agreement with the two ways of abandoning mentioned in the Abhidharma literature.

The first way mentioned is to abandon a certain phenomena by abandoning the nature of that phenomenon, by disconnecting from the attainment or acquisition of the nature of that phenomenon. This means that after abandoning that particular thing, an example could be delusion, then that delusion will not arise in the mind again. It has completely been abandoned. The second way of abandoning mentioned is to get rid of the attachment to that phenomenon, by getting rid of the attachment to it then you have abandoned the thing itself.

In some of the sutras mention is made of abandoning the eye or the ear. When we say that an Arhat has abandoned the eye, it does not mean one is without eyes, that after abandoning the eye, the eyes one has will cease to function. It means that the attachment to the inherent existence of eyes has been abandoned, as a result of which we can say that all the objects, such as the eyes, have been got rid of. Now in the case of self-grasping, if we say it has been abandoned, it means abandoned in the first manner, which is disconnecting from the attainment of the nature of the phenomena. This means that the phenomena itself does not remain and also that there is no other form of the nature of the phenomena, in terms of attainment or acquisition. This refers to the idea that when any state is experienced then another characteristic arises simultaneously, which is called acquisition. For example, when one generates bodhicitta, along with having bodhicitta, one also has the acquisition of the bodhicitta. So if one was to eliminate this bodhicitta, the first way of getting rid of it is to get rid of the acquisition of the bodhicitta. In the case of delusion, however, one does not have the delusion as well as its acquisition. So the second way of abandoning mentioned is that one has got rid of the attachment but the acquisition of the thing is still there.

In the case mentioned of an Arhat having eyes, this means one has the acquisition of the eyes. However, through getting rid of attachment to them, we can say one has abandoned the eyes. In the same way one can say one has attained enlightenment with regards to all phenomena. In the case of the Buddha Shakyamuni, when he became fully enlightened, this enlightenment deals directly with the knowledge of the one who has got enlightenment. But we also sometimes say that a Buddha, along with all phenomena has been enlightened. That is, to the transcendental knowledge of the Buddha, there is no difference in the ultimate emptiness and all phenomena. So the knowledge of ultimate emptiness, by which one is said to have been enlightened, is applicable to all phenomena. So the nature of all phenomena is realised, understood, as a result of which one has got enlightenment. Enlightenment applied to all phenomena. This is in the context of abandoning because when the grasping of attachment is abandoned, then the thing that is grasped at is said to have been abandoned. In regards to cause and result, these two things are different, coming one after another. In order to abandon the result, one has to find the source of the result and then abandon that. After that, there is no need to deal directly with the result. This is the reasoning behind the formulation of the second noble truth; the truth of the origin of suffering, this origin is that which is to be abandoned.

Now when we talk about suffering, it is divided into three: the suffering of suffering, the suffering of change, and the suffering of compositional factors. It is not only the feeling of suffering that one is talking about. What is generally believed to be happiness or pleasure is also a part of suffering or unsatisfactoriness because every aggregate which is defiled by any of the delusions is considered a deluded aggregate and whatever is a deluded aggregate is considered a source of suffering. Whether that deluded aggregate has the feeling of suffering, pleasure, or equanimity, it is considered an aggregate of suffering. Even if the being doesn't have the suffering of suffering, which is the usual suffering recognised as such even by the worldly mind, there may still be the suffering of change, which is usually interpreted as actual happiness in the worldly mind. Because it is not permanent and changes to suffering, this feeling of happiness itself is called the suffering of change. Anything, which is subject to impermanence, is called the suffering of compositional factors, or conditioned existence, which is a synonym for that which is impermanent.

So that which is subject to impermanence is also considered as an aggregate of suffering. This means that the effort to eliminate suffering is not only the path to be traversed. The purpose of the practise for a Mahayana practitioner is not only to get rid of the suffering as understood by the worldly mind or the suffering of samsara in general. The purpose is far beyond that; it is to get rid of all the aggregates of phenomena that are subject to impermanence. This means to transcend all types of suffering, as well as impermanence, which are the result of the mistaken or deluded mind. Now when one gets rid of this mistaken or deluded mind of the worldly nature, then there won't be these appearances of the suffering of suffering, of change and of compositional factors. The ultimate transcendental knowledge will become inseparable with the emptiness where not only the first two sufferings but also the suffering of conditioned existence is absent.

In the case of a Bodhisattva in meditative equipoise who has attained the first bhumi, one does not suffer as a worldly being would in the post-meditative session, still that Bodhisattva is subject to impermanence because he or she still comes under the law of change or impermanence. This state of being impermanent is also to be abandoned. Anyone who is subject to impermanence becomes an object of one of the three compassions. The first is the compassion of phenomena as the object, which is focussed on all sentient beings, all beings that are subject to impermanence. This includes even those

Bodhisattvas on the bhumis who are in the post-meditative session. The Bodhisattva who has attained meditative equipoise still returns to the worldly mind subject to impermanence because he or she has to come out of that meditation session and engages in activities in the post-meditative session.

However, when one remains in the meditative equipoise there is no grasping of any kind of impermanence. There is no grasping whatsoever, other than the understanding of the ultimate truth, in which the transcendental knowledge and the object of that knowledge have become inseparable. This means that the transcendental knowledge of the Bodhisattva can be said to be free from impermanence. Although the Bodhisattva still can come out of it. When in the meditative equipoise, knowledge has become inseparable from emptiness, so it is not subject to the suffering of impermanence. So, the one in meditative equipoise does not become an object of this first type of compassion.

In general, the suffering of conditioned existence or compositional factors includes all those who are subject to impermanence, as the state of being impermanent is not of the ultimate nature. One has to go beyond this state of impermanence and this is why it is mentioned as a form of suffering or unsatisfactoriness. As it is said in the text called the Uttaratantra, one of the five teachings of Maitreya Bodhisattva, 'In the relation to the three Jewels, when we talk about them as the objects of refuge, it is only the Jewel of Buddha which is the ultimate object of refuge.' The other two Jewels, the Dharma and the Sangha, are not ultimate objects of refuge for the following reasons. In the case of the Jewel of Dharma, it is said that even the Dharma of realisation, which refers to the different levels of understanding of the Bodhisattvas, is also not an ultimate object of refuge because they are of a deceptive nature, as they are of the nature of impermanence. In the case of the ultimate nature, which is emptiness, whether someone has proclaimed phenomena as empty of inherent existence or not, it always remains the same. There is no change in the nature of all phenomena. In the case of other phenomena, like the different levels of knowledge which are different forms of the mind, which are subject to impermanence, because of the nature of change, they are said to be of a deceptive nature and so cannot become the ultimate object of refuge. So, one reason to establish that the Jewel of Dharma is not the ultimate object of refuge is the reason that it is subject to impermanence. It is of an impermanent nature. So this means one has to go beyond this as well.

In the case of the Jewel of the Sangha, which refers to the Bodhisattvas on the path, they are not fully enlightened, they have not yet become accomplished realisers and there is still something they have to achieve. As such they don't possess omniscient knowledge and so they are not the ultimate object of refuge.

The truth of the origin of suffering includes all the delusions but the main example usually given is desire or attachment, this being explained in the context of a karma accompanied by the delusion of desire will definitely create a result. Although all the delusions can function as motivation, the main force comes from the delusion of craving, in a similar way to how it functions in the link of craving.

These first two noble truths are also called the two noble truths with respect to samsara. The truth of suffering includes all the aspects of samsara that are the result and truth of the origin of suffering includes all the aspects of samsara that are of the nature of cause. This is similar to how the twelve links of dependent arising are understood from the sequential order and in the reverse order. Through these two approaches one can know the nature of samsara from the aspect of cause and from the aspect of result.

Then we have the third noble truth, the truth of the cessation of suffering and the fourth, the truth of the path which leads to this cessation and these are called the two noble truths with respect to nirvana. The third and fourth noble truths similarly function as the result with respect to nirvana and the cause of nirvana, respectively.

The result is mentioned earlier because first one will come to know of the suffering, then naturally one will have a wish to get rid of that suffering and then one will attempt to find a way to get rid of it. Through one's investigations, one will come to know that delusions, such as craving, are the forces responsible, then one will naturally try to find ways to get rid of them. The final method to deal with them is the understanding of the ultimate nature, which is emptiness. As a result of this one will abandon the origin of suffering, which is the cause, then the sufferings will cease. This state of cessation of suffering is called the truth of cessation. This is the same as the state of nirvana, that which has gone beyond the state of suffering or sorrow. As soon as a practitioner attains the state of Arhatship, the Hinayana result, his knowledge of realising emptiness has got rid of the origin of suffering as well as the suffering of samsara itself.

The negation of the cause and result of samsara is called the actual state of nirvana, the actual state of cessation. What we consider as nirvana or the state of liberation is not actually the knowledge itself, it is not omniscient knowledge. In the case of the Buddha, the omniscient knowledge of a Buddha is not the state of cessation. The realisation, which is without all the faults and causes of samsara, is termed nirvana or cessation. Though it is linked with this knowledge it is not considered to be the knowledge itself.

To obtain this kind of state of cessation, one has to depend on the knowledge of realising emptiness during the course of the path and that knowledge by which one reaches the state of cessation is called the truth of the path. From a general point of view, the truth of the path includes all the five paths, which I have been explaining, and also with reference to how Avalokiteshvara answered Shariputra. The actual paths by which one obtains the state of cessation are the path of seeing and the path of meditation. The path of no-more learning is not considered as a cause because it is at the same level as when one attains the state of cessation, which means one has simultaneously developed omniscient knowledge.

Of these four noble truths, the first two and the fourth are of a relative nature; they refer to relative truth. The third, the path of cessation is considered as the ultimate truth, as it is not established on the basis of knowledge but on that which is free from all conceptual elaborations. In the text it is said that in emptiness 'there is no transcendental knowledge, no attainment and no non-attainment.' When the Bodhisattva on the path of meditation realises emptiness directly, that which is realised is not inherently existent, as all phenomena have been established as empty of inherent existence and this emptiness of inherent existence is what is realised directly by the transcendental knowledge.

Now one may think that this very knowledge, which realises emptiness, exists in some way. One may think that it exists inherently as otherwise one could not understand or realise this emptiness. One may think that it is necessary to establish the fact that emptiness is understood by someone or by the knowledge of emptiness itself. If one thinks that this knowledge is inherently existent, then this also needs to be discounted as invalid.

In order to establish this, the text states that in emptiness a Bodhisattva on the path of meditation does not even see the transcendental knowledge. The transcendental knowledge, which realises emptiness, is also called the transcendental knowledge of self-awareness. So this knowledge realises the emptiness and also realises itself. It is aware of the emptiness and of itself. Now when we say it is aware of itself or knows itself, then it would seem that the Bodhisattva on the path of meditation knows two different things through this transcendental knowledge. One is the emptiness and the other is the transcendental knowledge itself, which is not the same as emptiness and is of a relative nature.

However, in meditative equipoise, when a Bodhisattva sees something or realises something then that would be existent in ultimate truth, that which is inherently existent and that which is seen by transcendental knowledge in meditative equipoise comes to the same experience. This means that because nothing exists in ultimate truth the Bodhisattva in meditative equipoise does not see anything other than the emptiness of inherent existence. Now if the transcendent knowledge could see the knowledge itself, then by definition that knowledge would become inherently existent, as it is realised by the transcendental knowledge in meditative equipoise. So the point is that, although it is said to be self-aware, which means it realises itself, it does not realise itself in the form of a relative consciousness or knowledge.

The transcendental knowledge of a Bodhisattva and the ultimate emptiness have become inseparable, there is no difference between the understanding of emptiness and the understanding of the knowledge itself. So there is no contradiction in the sense that the transcendental knowledge will see two different things. It is aware of emptiness and of itself but there is no contradiction. Transcendental knowledge is understood in the same way as emptiness; in the state of enlightenment the omniscient knowledge of 'suchness' (*tathata*) and the omniscient knowledge of self-awareness are said to be of the same nature.

The Buddha said with regard to the third noble truth, "The truth of the cessation of suffering, this is something that one has to attain." This has to be understood in the relative context because in ultimate truth the Bodhisattva on the path of meditation does not realise or see anything that is of the nature of attainment. There isn't any form of attainment that exists inherently, which is why the text states that in emptiness 'there is no attainment and no non-attainment'.

The reason the text is formulated like this is to cover the circumstance of getting caught in a particular philosophical stance. For example, if the inherent existence of a certain phenomenon is to be negated and then after one comes to know of the negation of the inherent existence of that particular thing, one clings to the idea of the negation of that particular thing, then this is also a false notion, as it is not in agreement with the ultimate nature of that phenomena. After analysing, one has still not found anything of the nature of the existence of the phenomenon in question. One has established the state of negation but this state of negation should not be understood as inherently existent, so there is 'no non-attainment'. No state of negation in an inherent way in the ultimate viewpoint, as is understood by the transcendental knowledge of the Bodhisattva on the path of meditation.

So up to this point the method or practice of the Bodhisattva on the path of meditation is being explained. The text says that:

*Therefore, Shariputra, since Bodhisattvas have no attainment, they depend on the perfection of wisdom and abide in the perfection of wisdom. Since their minds have no obscurations, they have no fear. They have gone beyond all forms of errors or perversity and have attained the ultimate state of nirvana. All the Buddhas of the three times, have by depending on the perfection of wisdom fully realised the perfect, complete and unsurpassed state of enlightenment.*

From this point onwards, the answer given by Avalokiteshvara is in the context of the path of no-more learning. However, according to one way of explaining this text, up to 'they depend on the perfection of wisdom and abide in it,' refers to the last moment of the path of meditation, which means the Bodhisattva on the tenth bhumi, who remains absorbed in the vajra-like meditation (*vajropamasamadhi*). This is the last stage or level of the practice of a Bodhisattva after which, in the next moment, one will become an enlightened being. One will become a Buddha. The previous part of the text is based on the general nature of the path of meditation. Now this part of the text deals with the very last part of the path of meditation. As explained earlier, the path of meditation includes all the nine bhumis from the second to the tenth. Now generally, the object of relinquishment to be abandoned by the Bodhisattva on the path of meditation is called the obscuration of knowable object, which is the residue of the obscuration of delusion. The Bodhisattva has abandoned the obscuration of delusion on the first bhumi, through the path of seeing. This means one has abandoned the root, or the seed of these delusions. This is called the obscuration of knowable object because it does not obstruct one to go beyond samsara but it does obstruct the practitioner to attain the state of omniscience, the state of highest enlightenment. So there is a difference between the attainment that is just beyond samsara and the attainment that is beyond both samsara and nirvana.

The difference between the nirvana of a Hinayana Realiser (Shravaka and Pratyekabuddha Arhat), and the nirvana of a Mahayana Arhat, the *Samyak Sambuddha* (the perfectly Enlightened Buddha), is that the former state of liberation is beyond samsara but within nirvana, whereas the latter state of liberation has gone beyond both the limits of samsara and the nirvana realised by the Hinayana Arhat. In the case of Hinayana Arhats, as long as they remain in the state of nirvana, it is not beneficial to sentient beings as a whole. They have completely gone beyond samsara; this remaining in nirvana is not connected to those in samsara. Whereas a Buddha remaining in the state of enlightenment has gone beyond samsara, as one has got rid of all the faults of samsara but within that attainment of enlightenment, a Buddha emanates different forms to work for the sake of sentient beings. This is not just a state of liberation, a mere state of pacification of the faults of samsara. It is more than that. It is said to be the state of liberation, which does not abide in either extreme of samsara or nirvana. In this respect, the state of liberation (or enlightenment) of a Buddha is superior to the states of liberation of the Shravaka and Pratyekabuddha.

There are many objects of relinquishment that a practitioner still has to abandon before reaching the state of highest enlightenment. These are the objects of relinquishment that the Bodhisattva from the second to the tenth bhumi is abandoning, alongside the accumulation of merit through the activities of the six perfections and the practice of loving-kindness, compassion and bodhicitta.

While engaged in these activities in the post-meditative session and through the realisation of emptiness during meditative equipoise, the Bodhisattva will get rid of more and more of these residues of the delusions, which are called the obscurations of knowable object. This obscuration of knowable object is not only the residue of delusions but also takes the form of grasping. During the post-meditative session of a Bodhisattva traversing the ten bhumis, there is no 'true grasping' or the grasping of inherent existence but there is a grasping without the inherent existence. At this level, one grasps at phenomena but there is no grasping of them being inherently existent. Chandrakirti states in the Madhyamakavatara that everything is grasped at as inherently existent and that which falls within this grasping is called the relative truth. The word *samvriti* (relative truth) has the same meaning as ignorance, self-grasping or the grasping of true existence. A Bodhisattva on one of the ten bhumis does not possess this grasping of inherent existence. This ignorance that one has abandoned because it is the root cause of samsara and the result of which is that there is no grasping of any phenomenon as inherently existent. But still there is a grasping without inherent existence, the 'mere grasping of the characteristics of the phenomena.' This type of grasping is also to be abandoned in the course of the practice of the Bodhisattva on the bhumis. So this is also called 'the obscuration of knowable object' (*jneya varana*), the other obscuration being the obscuration of delusion, (*klesha varana*). There are two groups of objects of relinquishment, those relinquished through seeing and those relinquished through meditation. This mere grasping of the characteristics of phenomena will become the object of relinquishment through meditation.

When a Bodhisattva reaches the eighth bhumi he or she has got rid of even this 'mere grasping of phenomena'. Not only has one got rid of the 'true grasping' but the 'mere grasping of phenomena' has also been abandoned at the time of the eighth bhumi. What is left is the 'mere appearance of phenomena', which is also considered a result of a mistaken mind. Here we are not referring to the normal worldly mind but to a mind that is still not completely accomplished. As this mind has not attained the level of omniscient mind, there are still appearances as a result of this and these are the 'mere appearance of phenomena'. This is what is experienced during the last three bhumis as what is called 'dual appearance'.

There is the appearance of the grasped object and the

appearance of the grasping mind. This dual appearance is, of course, at the time of the post-meditative session and is also to be abandoned. This can be considered as a residue of both the obscurations of delusion and of knowable object. Then finally, through the vajra-like meditation of the Bodhisattva on the tenth bhumi, even this last residue of both the obscurations will be abandoned. All the grasping of inherent existence was already long abandoned but now even the grasping of mere appearance is no longer there. The dual appearance, which was there up to the tenth bhumi, has also been abandoned. So there won't be any dual appearance and there will be what is called complete absorption of the transcendental knowledge into the state of emptiness. Since, in the case of a Buddha, there is no coming out of the meditation session, then it will always be the same, which means that the transcendental knowledge or the mind of a Buddha always remains absorbed in the ultimate nature, which is emptiness, where there is no duality, or dual appearances.

These are the things that the Bodhisattvas traversing the nine bhumis will abandon, in the context of the path of meditation. These objects of relinquishment are divided into three main divisions and then each is divided further into three sub-divisions. So there are nine objects of relinquishment, which are abandoned by the Bodhisattvas on the nine bhumis, beginning with the Bodhisattva on the second bhumi to that on the tenth bhumi. The object of relinquishment is divided into three classes, the gross, the subtle and the subtlest. The gross part is also further divided into three called the gross gross, the subtle gross and the subtlest gross. In the same way the subtle and subtlest are also divided into these three parts giving us nine in all.

The grosser part of the object of relinquishment is abandoned during the lower bhumis. The Bodhisattva on the second bhumi will abandon the obscuration of knowable object that is classified as the gross part of gross, or gross gross. So it continues on until the Bodhisattva on the tenth bhumi will abandon the subtlest part of the subtle, which is in fact the last object of relinquishment, or abandonment. As far as the object of relinquishment is concerned, it starts with the gross part and ends with the very subtle part but in the case of the antidote, the knowledge of the Bodhisattva on the second bhumi is less refined or of an inferior nature to the knowledge of the Bodhisattva on the tenth bhumi. This means that knowledge of inferior quality can abandon an object of relinquishment of a greater, coarser degree, whereas in order to abandon an object of relinquishment of a smaller, finer degree, knowledge of superior quality is needed as an antidote.

One may postulate that this is not logically acceptable, because usually one will apply the stronger antidote in order to deal with the greater degree of object of relinquishment and one will only use a smaller degree of antidote to deal with a smaller type of object of relinquishment. Here it is the other way round; the tiniest, subtlest type of the object of relinquishment is abandoned by the most superior knowledge of a Bodhisattva, the knowledge of the tenth bhumi. This is logically established in the text by giving the example of washing clothes. To wash the gross, superficial dirt off the clothes, there is not much effort needed but to get rid of the subtle dirt, one needs to apply greater effort. One has to use soap or washing powder to deal with the subtle stains. In the same way it is reasonably proven regarding the knowledge acquired on the bhumis by Bodhisattvas with respect to dealing with the objects of relinquishment. So the explanations I have just been giving have been in reference to the part of the text which states, 'Therefore, Shariputra, since Bodhisattvas have no attainment, they depend on the perfection of wisdom and abide in the perfection of wisdom,' which is at the last moment of the level of the tenth bhumi Bodhisattva where one remains in the vajra-like meditation and is considered as the uninterrupted path of omniscient knowledge.

As already explained, there are two levels of the path of seeing. One is the uninterrupted path and the other is the released path or the liberated path. This division into two is applicable to all the paths. In the case of the path of no-more learning, the time of the vajra-like meditation is considered as the uninterrupted path of no-more learning. The next moment of the omniscient knowledge, the first moment of that, is considered the liberated path or the released path. The last moment of the knowledge of a Bodhisattva, who is remaining in the vajra-like meditation, is in the process of destroying the last object of relinquishment. So this knowledge is said to be capable of abandoning that last object of relinquishment. It is powerful enough to abandon that last object of relinquishment, but has not yet got rid of it, because it is in the process of 'fighting' with the object of relinquishment. So in this next moment the knowledge arises which can get rid of the last of it. This knowledge becomes omniscient knowledge. The first moment of omniscient knowledge is considered the liberated path of no-more learning.

On the path of no-more learning, there are no obscurations of delusion and knowable object which have not been completely abandoned, which means there is nothing to obstruct knowing or understanding something, whether it is in respect of understanding the ultimate truth from every aspect or whether it is to do with the understanding of any relative phenomenon. Now when it comes to the understanding of relative phenomenon, the omniscient knowledge that remains absorbed in the realisation of emptiness, does not itself realise or see the relative phenomenon. The same logical reasoning is applied here as to the omniscient knowledge of a Buddha in meditative equipoise. If the omniscient knowledge in meditative equipoise were to be aware of any phenomenon, then that phenomenon would become inherently existent. Through logical reasoning, nothing can be established as inherently existent, so no matter how omniscient a Buddha may be, one cannot see anything as inherently existent, because the idea of a Buddha being omniscient is not applicable to phenomena which do not exist in their ultimate nature. The Buddha is aware of, or knows, that thing which is there in the ultimate nature, which has a true nature. This means a Buddha is only aware of the state of emptiness of all phenomena. By being aware of, or realising only emptiness, it does not mean one always remains in some sort of negation, some sort of nothingness or a state out of which nothing arises.

Together with the accumulation of wisdom the Bodhisattva has also the accumulation of merit, in the form of the six perfections and engages in the generation of bodhicitta, loving-kindness and many varied activities to benefit sentient beings. As a result of the accomplishment of the practise of the realisation of emptiness, a Buddha has attained omniscient knowledge, by which one realises ultimate emptiness, the Formless Body which is a synonym for the Dharmakaya (the Body of Truth).

As a result of the accomplishment of the accumulation of merit, one attains the Form Body (*rupa kaya*), a synonym for the combination of the Nirmanakaya (the Body of Manifestation) and the Sambhogakaya (the Body of Enjoyment), which functions as a support to that transcendental knowledge and is endowed with the thirty-two major and eighty minor marks of a Buddha. From this, the different emanation forms arise, such as the supreme emanation form of Shakyamuni Buddha or skilful emanation forms in the form of different sentient beings. Examples such as in the form of a human being, an ordinary teacher or a skilful king of the rabbits, as exemplified in one of the Jataka Tales. These are considered skilful emanation forms. If a Buddha comes in an emanation form, it is not necessarily in the familiar human form of a Buddha. Three types of emanation forms are mentioned. The first is the skilful emanation in the form of inanimate objects, not in any form of living being. For example, coming in the form of a drum, a tree, or a bridge, which benefits sentient beings in various ways. Secondly, the birth emanation forms, which are the different forms of sentient beings, such as ordinary humans, animals and so on. Thirdly, the supreme emanation form refers to coming in the form of a Buddha, such as the case of Buddha Shakyamuni. He is an emanation form of Buddha in the form of the Enjoyment Body. The attainment of enlightenment by the Buddha Shakyamuni is not the first attainment of enlightenment; it is, as it is said in the Mahayana scriptures, only one manifestation. There have been Buddhas in the past, prior to Shakyamuni and there will be Buddhas in the future. These manifestations are within the activity of supreme emanation forms, whereas, if a Buddha comes in the form of an ordinary human being, an ordinary teacher, or any other sentient being, that is considered an emanation of birth. So through these different ways of emanating, a Buddha will continuously work for the benefit of sentient beings. All these emanations happen while the Buddha is continuously absorbed in the realisation of ultimate emptiness.

When in the context of foundation, or ground, we refer to the philosophical tenet that states, 'When emptiness is acceptable, everything is acceptable'; this fact is applicable now, at the time of result. As the Buddha is continuously absorbed in ultimate emptiness, then all activities can be performed, in the relative, for the sake of sentient beings. The combination of the two truths is applicable with respect to all three stages, the foundation, the path and the result. So while emptiness is being explained, the relative component is also implicitly expressed. At the time of the path of no-more learning, the meditative equipoise of the Buddha, in which there is only the realisation of emptiness, the Buddha still emanates in different forms. Not only in the three emanation forms I mentioned, which manifest here on the earth but travelling to the Buddha realms, in the form of the Enjoyment Body, the Buddha also benefits Bodhisattvas on the different bhumis by giving Mahayana teachings there.

With respect to the practise of perfection of wisdom by a Mahayana practitioner, one will, in this way, attain the complete enlightenment in the form of becoming a Buddha. Up to this point, the answers given by Avalokiteshvara are meant for those who are of inferior or lower mental faculties. The way of practising the perfection of wisdom is explained extensively, applying it to all the five paths. This is followed by the answer given for those of higher or more acute mental faculties. Avalokiteshvara continues:

*Therefore, it is the mantra of perfection of wisdom, the mantra of great knowledge, the unsurpassed mantra, the unequalled mantra, the mantra which pacifies all kinds of sufferings. It is not false, so it should be understood as a true aspect.*

All these qualities or attributes related to mantra are referring to this mantra of Prajnaparamita, the mantra of the perfection of wisdom:

*The Prajnaparamita mantra is proclaimed here and is recited thus: Tadyatha Om gate gate paragate parasamgate bodhi svaha.*

Then Avalokiteshvara continues:

*Thus, Shariputra, a Bodhisattva Mahasattva, should engage in the practise of this profound perfection of wisdom."*

This is the explanation or answer given to the question of

Shariputra in the context of those of higher mental faculties. This means that the same type of teaching that was given earlier in the context of the five paths is also to be found in this mantra of the perfection of wisdom, the Prajnaparamita mantra. In the context of Vajrayana, when the meaning of the word mantra is explained, it is that which has the capability of protecting the mind from characteristics. That which protects the mind from characteristics is called a mantra.

Now these characteristics can be of many types, ranging from the characteristics of ordinary phenomena, or ordinary being, to the grasping of dual appearances. In the case of Vajrayana, the practise of the visualisation of a deity, the process of creation in which you visualise all things as deities (*utpattikrama, bkyed rim*), also has this meaning of mantra because it protects the mind from grasping ordinary characteristics. Before this, one only has the view of everything as ordinary, as seen by the worldly mind. Now through this visualisation of deities, the way of looking at all things in an ordinary way will be abandoned. In the same way, this mantra of the perfection of wisdom protects the mind from the grasping of different levels of characteristics, from grasping the inherent characteristic; from grasping the mere characteristic; then protecting the mind from dual appearances. All those objects of relinquishment that were explained earlier are to be abandoned through this practise of this perfection of wisdom. So this mantra that is given here has the capability of protecting the mind from all these objects of relinquishment or facilitates the mind to abandon them. The mind becomes enlightened due to being protected from these types of grasping. For these reasons it is called a mantra.

It is called the mantra of great knowledge because the perfection of wisdom, the knowledge of realising emptiness is the greatest knowledge. There is no knowledge greater than this. It is called the unsurpassed mantra because there is nothing that can surpass this knowledge, nothing superior to it. It is the unequalled mantra, as there is nothing equal to the level of this mantra; it is equal only to itself. In other words it is matchless with respect to other knowledge or other types of practice. It is the mantra of pacifying all sufferings, as through this practice of this mantra one will get rid of all the sufferings of samsara.

'It is not of a false nature', meaning this mantra of the perfection of wisdom is not a deceptive factor, or false knowledge, so one can perceive this as a true form of knowledge or true practice. By saying that it is 'true', does not mean it should be considered as inherently or truly existent but in a relative sense differentiating between false and true or unmistaken knowledge, then the perfection of wisdom is to be considered true knowledge. So when the text says, *'The Prajnaparamita mantra is proclaimed here and is recited thus'*; this means that the mantra itself expresses the same teachings extrapolated earlier.

The first word of the mantra, the Sanskrit word *Tadyatha* means it is so, it is as follows, or it is like this, referring to the perfection of wisdom through which a Bodhisattva engages being like this. This is also an answer to the question put by Shariputra in the beginning, where he said that, "How should a son or daughter of noble lineage train, who wishes to engage in the practise of the perfection of wisdom?" So it is like this that one can engage in this type of practice.

*Om* is not a part of the practice; it is in fact a syllable which one finds in the beginning of all mantras. In Vajrayana most of the mantras have the syllable *Om* at the beginning. There are some cases where it is not there but many scholars say that it should be added, as it is implied. So it is added in many cases. Even in the case of this mantra in some other versions the *Om* is omitted but generally, as far as Tibetans recite it, it is included. So it is at the beginning of a mantra and is said to symbolise the body, speech and mind, represented by the three sounds A, U, and M - AUM, but pronounced *Om*. So the one who will be engaged in the full practice should be engaged through all their body, speech and mind. The actual meaning of the word mantra is explained as the protection for the mind. Through this protection, the body and speech are also protected.

*Gate* in Sanskrit means to go. So literally it means, go, go. The first *gate* refers to the practice of the path of accumulation, to proceed in the path of accumulation, which includes all the practices mentioned earlier about understanding the emptiness of five aggregates through study and contemplation. Go and engage in the practice of realisation of emptiness through study and contemplation.

The second *gate* refers to the practice at the time of the path of application. Go and engage in the practice of realisation of emptiness through meditation.

Then, *para* means well or perfectly, so *paragate* means go perfectly and is applicable to the practice at the time of the path of seeing. So this comes after the practice of the path of application, which although it is a practice of the realisation of emptiness through meditation it is still only conceptual. But now, one is on the real path to Buddhahood, one is perfectly going. Going perfectly reveals the practice that a Bodhisattva on the path of seeing should engage in, which is the direct realisation of a Buddha, the direct realisation of emptiness.

*Parasamgate*, translates as 'perfectly and completely go.' This refers to the practice at the time of the path of meditation. Here, the Bodhisattva is not only engaged perfectly through a direct realisation of emptiness but one is completing the journey to the state of Buddhahood.

*Bodhi* refers to the 'state of enlightenment'. This refers to the path of no-more learning. There is the non-dual attainment of the state of realisation of emptiness, which is the accumulation of wisdom (*prajna, ye shes*) and the accomplishment of the method aspect, the understanding of all skilful methods of benefiting sentient beings (*upaya, thabs*), which is the accumulation of merit.

*Svaha* is how almost all mantras are concluded. It is usually translated as 'this is how the foundation is built.' So, for example, *gate* refers to the practise of the path of accumulation. This practice should be built as a foundation. All these practices have to be built in a solid way; each preceding practice will then become the foundation for the next. 'In this way, the great Bodhisattvas should engage in the profound perfection of wisdom.' This refers to those Bodhisattvas with the higher level of mental faculties being able to engage in the profound perfection of wisdom in this way.

*Question:* Could you explain about the thirty-two and eighty marks of a great being?

*Answer:* Both the Sambhogakaya and the Nirmanakaya emanations have these marks. The original marks are those of the Sambhogakaya level, the marks of the Nirmanakaya are a manifestation of those.

*Question:* What is the difference between four Bodies and three Bodies' formulation?

*Answer:* Four Bodies is explained mainly in the context of Vajrayana. Even some scholars in the Sutrayana accept the idea of four Bodies. In the Prajnaparamita literature, many different commentaries arose on the text called the Abhisamayalamkara. Two systems developed, one states that the text itself reveals four Bodies, while the other system says it only reveals three Bodies. There is a difference that arises from the interpretation of one verse of that text, in fact.

In the Sutrayana tradition, the Sakya interpretation, along with most other schools, believe in the three-Body formulation. Svabhavikakaya, the Body of Essence or Nature, is not separately established in the sutras. The four Bodies' formulation comes when the transcendental knowledge is divided into two, nature and knowledge. At the time of attainment it is inseparable but we can separate its aspects, there is no mention of this in the sutras, it comes in Vajrayana.

*Question:* So when it is divided into two how is it labelled?

*Answer:* Svabhavikakaya and Dharmakaya.

*Question:* Normal practitioners can only see Buddha in the form of Nirmanakaya; can they not see the Sambhogakaya?

*Answer:* No, only Bodhisattvas on the bhumis can.

*Question:* It has been said that all the Vajrayana teachings were given by Buddha in the form of Vajradhara, so does that mean that there were originally only given to Bodhisattvas?

*Answer:* We can say that this is one of the differences between Sutrayana and Vajrayana. We cannot all come to the same conclusion. The final attainment, in the form of Buddhahood is usually explained as being the same, whether one describes it as the Buddha of the eleventh bhumi or Vajradhara of the thirteenth bhumi, there is no difference in the nature of the result. However, the method is of a different nature.

The next section is the approval of the Buddha of the reply given by Avalokiteshvara:

*Then the Victorious One came out of the absorption of profound illumination and said to Bodhisattva Arya Avalokiteshvara,*

## 'JOYOUS ELEGANT SPEECH'

*"Good, it is well done, son of lineage, it is as you have replied. The practise of the perfection of wisdom is as you have explained and the son or daughter of lineage should engage in the practise in just this way and all the Tathagatas will rejoice."*

As mentioned earlier, the dialogue between Shariputra and Avalokiteshvara was blessed and empowered by the Buddha, which means the reply given by Avalokiteshvara was the same as if it had been spoken by the Buddha himself. This section is to demonstrate this. However, this does not mean that there is an occasion when the Buddha comes out of absorption and remains in the post-meditative state. As it was explained earlier, one of the exclusive attributes of the Buddha is that one always remains absorbed in the meditation of emptiness. So this coming out of absorption is an outward activity for some of his students, for example, Avalokiteshvara. The Buddha has different ways or levels of performing activities for the benefit of sentient beings.

Whether one is referring to the beginning, middle or end of this Heart Sutra, the Buddha remains in continual absorption, as far as the actual realisation of emptiness goes. To different disciples, the Buddha may be seen to be engaged in different activities in accordance with their vision or intellect. All outward activities are explained as the result of the accomplishment of merit, which arise when the karmic link from the disciple's side is ripened. The state of enlightenment is in the meditative equipoise of remaining in the ultimate nature but the outward appearances may vary from disciple to disciple. In this case, it is said that to the general disciples, the Buddha was seen to be abiding at Vulture's Peak in a normal way. The Buddha being seen to be in the absorption called 'profound illumination' and his body radiating brilliant light is said to have been perceived by only a few disciples, such as Avalokiteshvara.

These differences in the perception of the Buddha amounts

to the same thing as the differences between the Sambhogakaya form of the Buddha, visible to the Bodhisattvas on the bhumis and the Nirmanakaya form of the Buddha, visible to all types of disciples, whether they have entered any of the three vehicles or not. So only those of a higher level experienced this entering and coming out of the absorption of Profound Illumination, this entering and coming out is only an outward appearance. There is no point when the Buddha comes out of the ultimate meditation on emptiness. The approval by the Buddha confirms that the teaching given by Avalokiteshvara was the same as a Buddha would have given. Hence, the Buddha did not add anything or make any changes.

The statement that, 'All the Tathagatas will rejoice', is explained in two ways: Firstly, as the answer given is in agreement with the actual nature of reality, the perfect explanation, then all the Buddhas of the ten directions and the three times will also rejoice. The teaching given by one Buddha will not be different from the teaching given by another Buddha. Secondly, when a son or daughter of the lineage is engaged in the practise in the way Avalokiteshvara described, then all the Tathagatas will rejoice. In this case the admiration will be directed towards the practitioner. This concludes the section of the approval by the Buddha of the answer given by Avalokiteshvara.

The final section is the assembly of disciples being pleased with the teaching of the Buddha; they take to their hearts what Buddha said:

*After the Victorious One said thus, the Venerable Shariputra, the great Bodhisattva Arya Avalokiteshvara, all the assembly of human disciples, devas, asuras and gandharvas, rejoiced and admired what had just been taught and praised by the Buddha.*

This concludes the commentary on the Heart Sutra.

When the Heart Sutra is recited, it is usually accompanied by a method for overcoming obstacles. After the recitation of the Sutra itself, the mantra is recited three, seven, twenty-one times or whatever is possible. Then, another prayer is done three times, with the clapping of hands at specific points. This is a common ritual to overcome obstacles. There is an account of the god Indra, who is the king of the Thirty-third Heaven, who, when there was an imminent attack from the asuras and his life was in danger, he remembered about the Heart Sutra, which he recited and prayed accordingly. As a result of this, the hatred in the minds of the demi-gods diminished and they did not come to attack. Through the chanting of the Sutra and the prayer, the obstacle was overcome. It is said in the prayer:

*Just as Indra, king of the gods, through the chanting of this Sutra and contemplating its meaning, was able to overcome external obstacles, then in the same way, through the chanting of this Sutra and contemplating its meaning, may I also be able to overcome all types of obstacles.*

When one has a specific obstacle, then at this time one can concentrate on this, but generally we recite the prayer to remove all obstacles for oneself and for all sentient beings.

*Question:* So can we use this mantra on a daily basis along with our other practices?

*Answer:* Yes, as you have now received the textual transmission. Usually, there is no need for any other initiation.

*Question:* Could you describe the visualisation one should generate during the recitation of the Sutra and during the prayer at the end of the Sutra?

*Answer:* There is no special visualisation mentioned, other than setting one's mind on the overcoming of obstacles. However, if one were to be more elaborate, then one could start with taking refuge, followed by generating bodhicitta, in which case there is a visualisation:

On a jewelled throne supported by eight lions, generate a lotus seat, on top of which is a moon and sun disc. Shakyamuni Buddha is seated on these, in the form of a bikshu. At his heart level, visualise a lotus seat, moon and sun discs, on top of which is seated the Devi Bhagavati Prajnaparamita, the Mother Perfection of Wisdom. She is the embodiment of the transcendental knowledge of all the Buddhas. Visualise this female deity with one face and four arms. The outer right hand holds a vajra, the outer left hand holds a text of Prajnaparamita, while the two inner hands are in the mudra of meditation. At the heart level of Bhagavati Prajnaparamita, visualise a bija - seed syllable - HUNG surrounded by the letters of the mantra cycling in a clockwise direction. So this is the visualisation.